Training Skiing

This book was given to me by: SEAN + Melissa

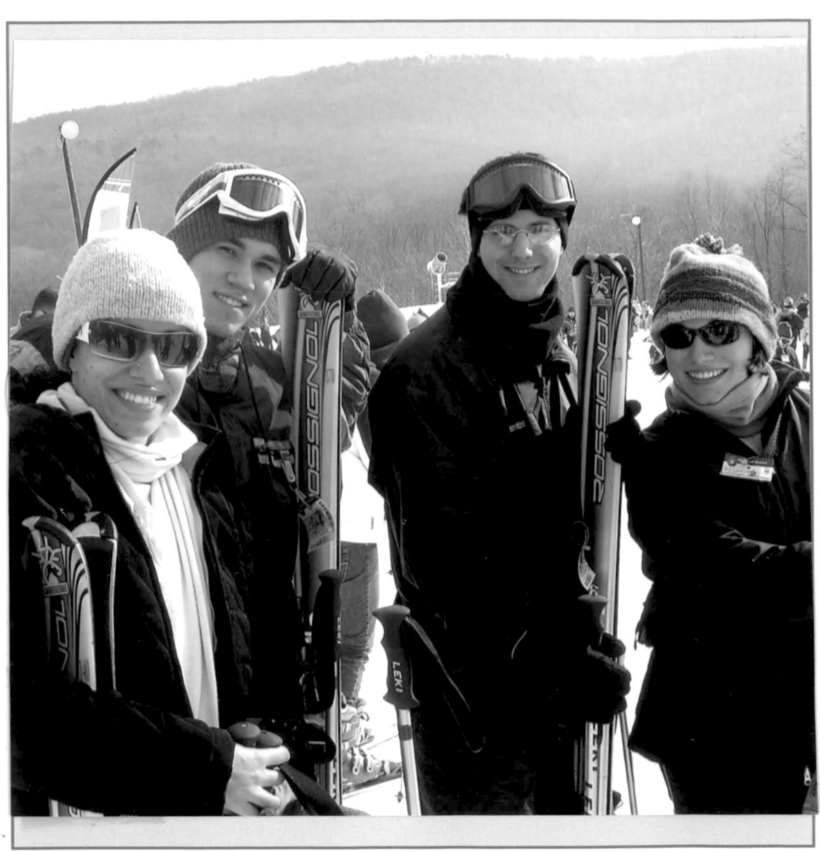

My name: ______________________

My birthday: ______________________

My address: ______________________

____

TRAINING SKIING

Katrin Barth/Hubert Brühl

Sports Science Consultant:
Dr. Berndt Barth

Meyer & Meyer Sport

The authors would like to thank Franz J. Ringsgwandl, DSV-Juniors Trainer, for his technical advice.

British Library Cataloguing in Publication Data
A catalogue record for this book is available from the British Library

Training Skiing
Katrin Barth / Hubert Brühl
Oxford: Meyer & Meyer Sport (UK) Ltd., 2006
ISBN-10: 1-84126-174-2
ISBN-13: 978-1-84126-174-4

Aachen, Adelaide, Auckland, Budapest, Graz, Johannesburg,
New York, Olten (CH), Oxford, Singapore, Toronto
Member of the World
Sports Publishers' Association (WSPA)
www.w-s-p-a.org
Printed and bound by: TZ Verlag, Germany
ISBN-10: 1-84126-174-2
ISBN-13: 978-1-84126-174-4
E-Mail: verlag@m-m-sports.com

.... TABLE OF CONTENTS

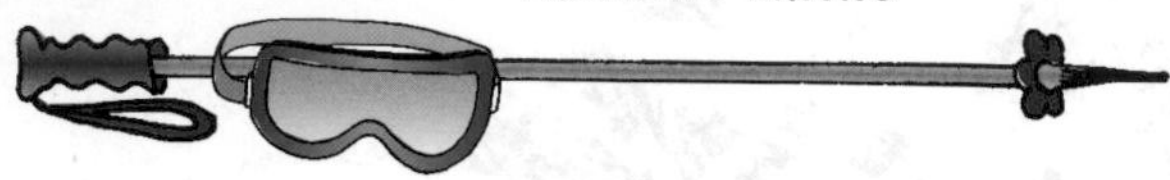

Caution:

The exercises and practical suggestions in this book have been carefully chosen and reviewed by the authors. However, the authors are not liable for accidents or damages of any kind incurred in connection with the content of this book.

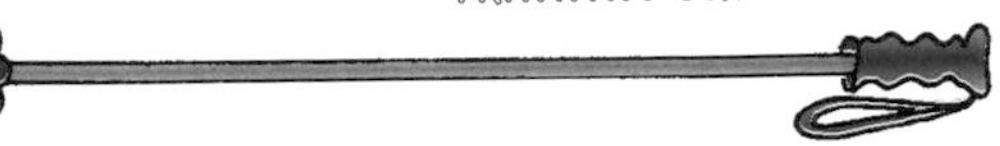

HELLO, IT'S ME, SNOWMAN!
MAY BE YOU EVEN REMEMBER ME FROM
THE BOOK "LEARNING SKIING". SO NOW
YOU WANT TO GET SERIOUS ABOUT
TRAINING? OKAY, I'M WITH YOU!

HI THERE, SKI-NUT! I AM BABY SKITTY,
SNOWMAN'S FRIEND, AND OF COURSE
I'M ALONG FOR THE RIDE AGAIN! IN FACT,
I WOULDN'T MISS IT! I HAVE LOTS OF
TRAINING TIPS FOR YOU!

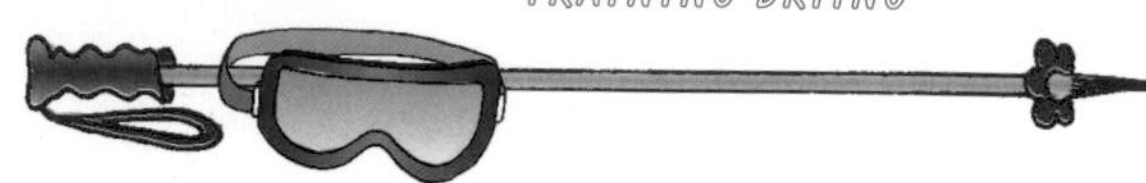

IN THE BOOK, YOU WILL OFTEN SEE SOME PICTURES OF SNOWMAN.

When you see this gesture, it means that Snowman has a great tip for you. He will make suggestions or point out mistakes.

Here are brain teasers or riddles. You can find the answers and solutions in the back of the book.

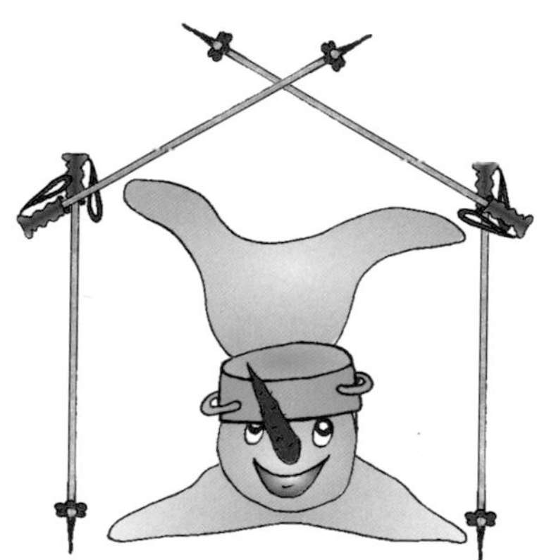

This figure means there are exercises that can be done at home.

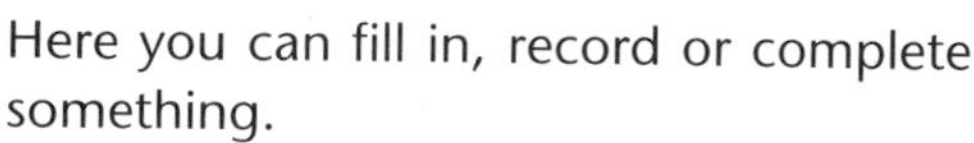

Here you can fill in, record or complete something.

. . . . 1 DEAR SKIER

For many children, adolescents and adults, skiing is one of the best recreational activities in winter. The exercise in the fresh, crisp winter air simply feels good and is healthy. For many children, especially in mountain regions, skiing is taken for granted. You have to be able to do it, just like walking, swimming or riding a bike. Surely you, too, have learned to ski for that reason, and by now you have taken many a run. Maybe you even learned with the help of our book, *Learning Skiing*, and are already familiar with such a book.

So if you are now interested in this training book and you are reading it, we can assume that alpine skiing as a recreational activity is not enough or you. You enjoy this sport, want to continue and train seriously. You want to refine your technique, improve your condition and successfully participate in races. You want to be fast and win.

Most likely you are already involved in a sport or are in a ski club, and are training with children your age under the direction of experienced trainers or ski instructors.

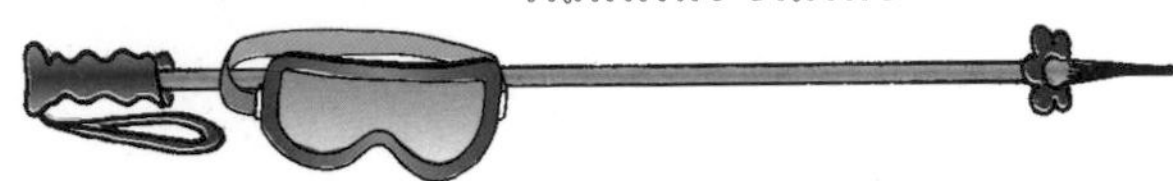

Before we begin, a short story:

A strapping boy was visiting the mountains and wanted to climb a high peak. Cheerfully he packed food and drink and started to hike with a bounce in his step. Since he wasn't familiar with the route, he made slow progress. He climbed up and when he realized that he couldn't get any further he had to turn back and start over. These detours cost him lots of strength. Sometimes he got lucky and found a trail that brought him a little closer to the top. After many such attempts he finally reached the summit only to realize that others were already there. They told him about a good hiking trail. He could have taken that without all of those detours.

Why didn't he use a map or ask someone who had already taken this hike?

Ski training is similar to our story about the "conqueror of the peak." Many skiers before you have trained and some have become very successful. So you don't need to reinvent skiing and ski training, but rather learn from the experience of skiers before you. That will make it much easier for you to learn.

The book *Training Skiing* is a kind of "trail map" and a small tutorial on how to climb that "skier's peak" without taking many detours. And, of course, you have your trainer who can show you the right way.

Sometimes it happens that experienced skiers, trainers and book writers have different opinions about training. That is normal. Ask if you are not clear on something and find out the reasons behind different opinions.

If by chance we did make a mistake or development has simply advanced, you can take notes directly in your book.

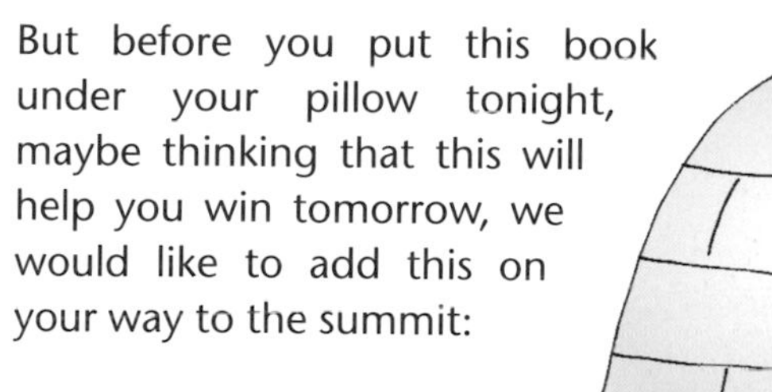

But before you put this book under your pillow tonight, maybe thinking that this will help you win tomorrow, we would like to add this on your way to the summit:

We want to offer you advice and explain how you can train correctly. But you must do the training. Whether or not you reach the summit is mostly up to you.

Anything in this book pertaining to training is for girls, as well as for boys. But to keep it simple we will refer to skiers or athletes in general. Of course, trainer or ski instructor also refers to female trainers and ski instructors.

We hope you have lots of fun with this book. It will definitely provide you with lots of interesting information to accompany you on a hopefully quick and safe road to the "summit." We wish you lots of success!

The authors, Snowman, and Skitty

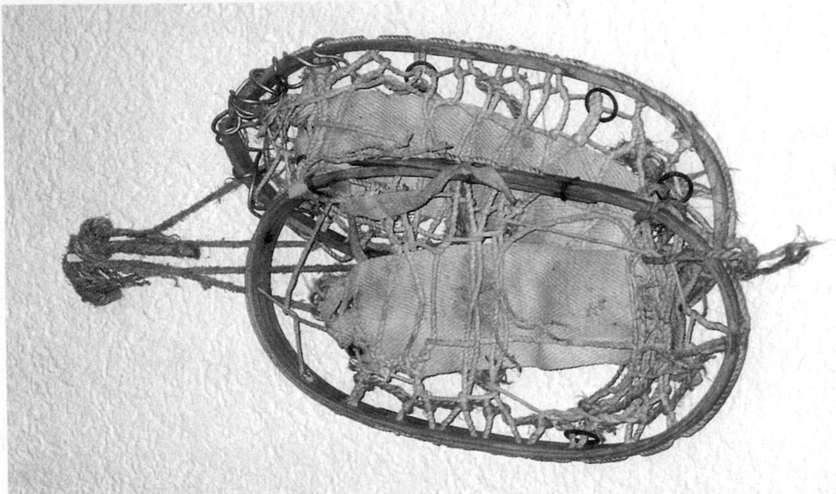

These are snowshoes like the ones people wore in ancient times on long treks and while hunting in the snow.

Wooden skis with bindings made from leather straps. The poles are made from bamboo.

. . . . 2 FROM WOODEN SKI TO RACING SKI

Which nation discovered skiing? Who built the first skis?

Was it the Native Americans, the northern Germanic tribes or Stone Age man in what is now the Sahara? Of course, nobody knows for sure, but they were definitely people who wanted to move about and survive in the snow.

Snowshoes were woven from twigs and sticks, or constructed from hewn pieces of wood. Thus, people did not have to wade through the snow, but were able to move more quickly, and consequently were able to hunt more successfully.

It did not take long until people also began to enjoy the movement and fast downhill gliding on skis. Maybe they even had small races. Of course, the material and the technology continually changed and especially improved. And that continues today!

Sometimes you still see old snowshoes, skis or poles as decorations in ski lodges or at lift stations.

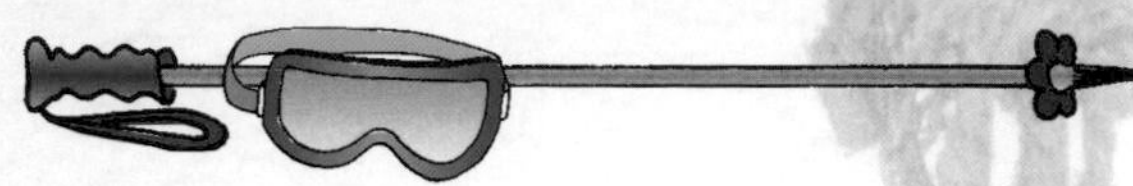

DID YOU KNOW ...

... THAT ANCIENT ROCK DRAWINGS HAVE BEEN DISCOVERED, DEPICTING HUNTERS ON SKIS HUNTING REINDEER? THE FIRST STONE AGE DRAWINGS DATE BACK TO THE YEAR 4000 B.C..

... THAT PEOPLE IN NORTHERN EUROPE REVERED SKI GODS? THERE WAS ULL OR ULLR, NAMES THAT MANY TOWNS IN NORWAY STILL CARRY TODAY. SCANDINAVIA WAS EVEN NAMED AFTER THE SKI GODDESS SKADI.

... THAT THE FAMOUS NORWEGIAN POLAR EXPLORER FRIDTJHOF NANSEN WAS THE FIRST TO CROSS GREENLAND IN 1888/1889? HE AND HIS COMPANIONS WERE EXPERIENCED SNOW-SHOERS, AND WERE ABLE TO MOVE QUITE WELL ON SKIS. BACK THEN HIS BOOK ABOUT THE EXPEDITION IMPRESSED MANY PEOPLE AND MOTIVATED THEM TO START SKIING.

... THAT THE FIRST HOLMENKOLLEN SKI GAMES TOOK PLACE IN 1892? THAT FIRST YEAR THE ONLY COMPETITIONS OFFERED WERE IN SKI JUMPING AND 30-KM CROSS-COUNTRY SKIING, TO THE REJOICING OF THE MANY SPECTATORS.

... THAT AROUND 1800, SKIING WAS A TRADITION IN THE TELEMARK REGION AND WAS EXECUTED IN VARIOUS FORMS AND WITH GREAT SKILL? FROM THERE IT SPREAD ALL OVER NORWAY. TELEMARK IS STILL A CONCEPT TODAY.

... THAT JOHANN FRIEDRICH GUTSMUTHS, THE FOUNDER OF MODERN PHYSICAL EDUCATION IN SCHOOLS AROUND 1800, WAS A SKIER HIMSELF, AND THAT HE RECOMMENDED SKIING AS A VALUABLE FORM OF PHYSICAL TRAINING? THIS MADE HIM THE ORIGINATOR OF SKIING IN GERMANY.

... THAT THE FIRST SKI LIFT IN THE WORLD WAS CONSTRUCTED IN SCHOLLACH (BLACK FOREST REGION) IN 1908? THIS TOW LIFT WAS APPROXIMATELY 600 YARDS LONG, AND SURMOUNTED A DIFFERENCE IN ELEVATION OF APPROXIMATELY 82 FEET.

... THAT THE FIRST STEEL EDGES WERE DEVELOPED BY RUDOLF LETTNER AROUND 1925? IN SUBSEQUENT YEARS THESE BECAME VERY IMPORTANT FOR ALPINE SKIERS.

... THAT IN 1930, AT THE REQUEST OF SWITZERLAND, THE FIS DECIDED TO INCLUDE DOWNHILL AND SLALOM IN THEIR OFFICIAL COMPETITIONS? THIS MARKED THE BREAKTHROUGH OF ALPINE COMPETITIVE SPORTS.

... THAT ONLY AT THE FIFTH OLYMPIC WINTER GAMES IN 1948, IN SAINT MORITZ, WERE ALPINE INDIVIDUAL EVENTS (DOWNHILL AND SLALOM) FOR MEN AND WOMEN ON THE PROGRAM?

... THAT THE DEVELOPMENT OF THE CARVING TECHNIQUE AND THE CORRESPONDING CARVING SKIS ONLY BEGAN ABOUT 30 YEARS AGO?

THE EVOLUTION OF ALPINE SKIING TECHNIQUE

The skier Matthias Zdarsky from Lilienfeld, Germany, recognized that the Norwegian skiing technique was not suitable for the high mountains of the Alps. So in 1896, he wrote a book titled *Lilienfeld Alpine Skiing Technique*. This was probably the first skiing tutorial. Zdarsky invents the *rigid binding* and develops *shorter skis without a directional groove*. He introduces the *stem turn*.

The skiers were able to break by doing the so-called "plough." The bamboo pole without the basket was also suitable for testing the snow consistency.

Practical ski attire for female downhill skiers was unfortunately not customary in 1900.

The long dresses probably acted more like a brake!

THIS IS HOW THE SPORT OF SKIING IS ORGANIZED

Most athletes who train in skiing are members of a ski club. There, the athletes have the best training conditions, certified trainers, and are well cared for. Getting ready for an athletic competition and starting on the team together with your buddies is fun.

What is the name of your club? Write it down here and draw or paste the logo and team colors in the box.

My club:

____

____

Logo:

Every country has a ski association for its athletes.

Do you know the name of the ski association in your country? Write it down here.

____

____

Logo:

Ski associations support the various clubs, make sure the ski instructors and trainers are well trained, look after the top athletes and organize competitions and championship events in the individual disciplines. In addition, they look after the recreational athletes, support work done in the ski areas and organize competitions for children.

THIS IS HOW THE SPORT OF SKIING IS ORGANIZED ON AN INTERNATIONAL LEVEL

The worldwide federation for all ski athletes is called the **Fédération International de Ski** (**FIS** in short).

FIS was founded in 1924 at the first Olympic Winter Games in Chamonix, France. It has been based in Oberhofen, Switzerland for many years.

All national ski associations are members of FIS. Currently, there are 103 worldwide. There are committees for alpine skiing, cross-country skiing, Nordic Combined, ski jumping, freestyle and snowboarding. In addition, there are sub-committees.

The sub-committees' functions are:

- Decisions regarding rules, materials and dates.
- Responsibility for awarding and implementing the major World Cup races.
- Continued development and modernization of the established competitive disciplines in skiing and snowboarding.

FIS is organizer of the skiing and snowboarding World Championships, and is in charge of the skiing and snowboarding competitions at the Olympics.

If you want to know more, look on the Internet:

www.fis-ski.com

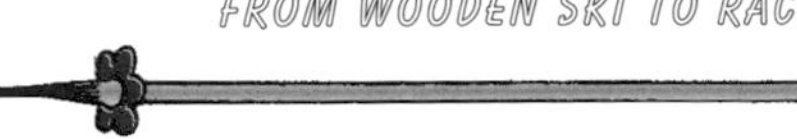

List of champions

Follow the next World Championships (WCH) and Olympic Games (OG). On this page, you can record the names of the current world champions and Olympic champions.

Women	WCH 2_ _ _ in	OG 2_ _ _ in ....
Downhill		
Slalom		
Giant Slalom		
Super-G		

Men	WCH 2_ _ _ in	OG 2_ _ _ in ....
Downhill		
Slalom		
Giant Slalom		
Super-G		

Use a pencil or copy this chart if you also want to record the results of the next World Championships or Olympic Games!

You can also follow other championship events and World Cups to document the results.

Sport and art

Sports and athletes are popular themes with many artists. The elegance of movement, the beauty of their bodies, their speed and their power inspired many paintings, drawings, sculptures and photos.

Have you ever seen such a piece of sport art? Pay attention the next time you are in a public building or a museum.

We really like this picture showing an alpine skier. It is a serigraph by American artist LeRoy Neiman; it is called "Stenmark," was created in 1980 and the size of the original is 38" x 24"

. . . . 3 HI THERE, MONIKA!

Monika Bergmann-Schmuderer
Born on April 17, 1978, in Neunkirchen, Bavaria
Occupation: Chief Customs Officer

Hi there, Moni! What do you think is so great about skiing?

Skiing is just plain fun and anyone can learn this sport. Young or old, it doesn't matter! You are out moving in the fresh air and can enjoy the mountains and the snow. And if the sun is shining, it is a perfect winter day.

Which talents does a good skier need to have?

A skier needs to have a good sense of movement, coordination and endurance. But all the talent in the world is useless without diligent training. Success can only be achieved through lots and lots of practice, even if it is less fun on some days.

Do you sometimes not feel like training? What do you do then?

Of course I don't feel like working sometimes! I think that happens to everyone. That's when you just have to pull yourself up by the bootstraps and train anyway. I want to be successful in racing, and I still have many goals. I can't afford to fall behind in my training.

What are your goals?

As long as I stay fit and healthy, I continue to set new and bigger goals for myself.

What were your favorite and most important successes?

Amongst those are winning the Junior World Championship in 1997, the good placement at the Olympics and placing in the World Cup. Of course, I am very happy about becoming the 2004 German Slalom champion.

What does the sport of skiing mean to you?

Right now, training and racing are very important. I still have big plans. But I also know that my career as a competitive athlete will be over some day.

That is why I never neglected my education and learned an occupation. A good education is important for the future.

Surely skiing is your favorite hobby! Do you have any other interests?

Of course – anyone who wants to be successful obviously has to train a lot! But time with my husband and two cats is also important to me. Besides that I like going to the movies to see the newest film.

What advice do you have for young athletes?

You have to believe in yourself, never give up and have fun doing it. If you approach the task at hand with fun and joy, sooner or later you will be successful.

How can someone find out more about you?

Look at my homepage; there is lots of information, nice photos and current topics. There you can also send me a message or chat with me online.

Homepage: www.monika-bergmann.de

Thank you very much for this conversation, and good luck in the future!

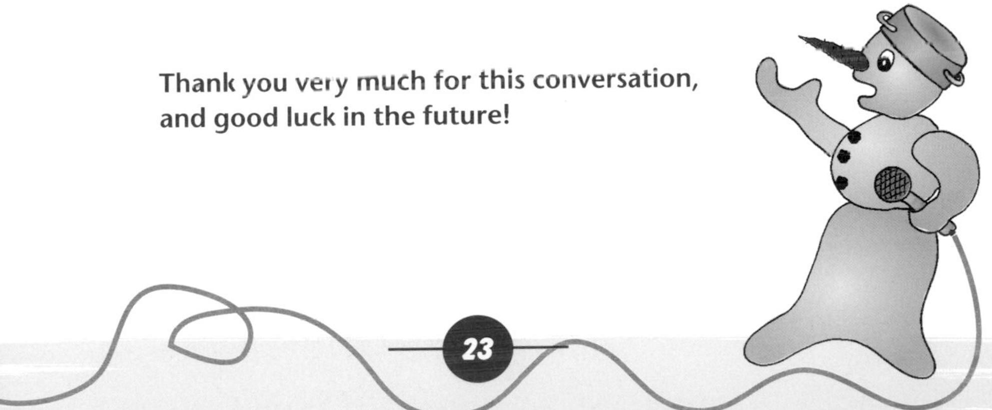

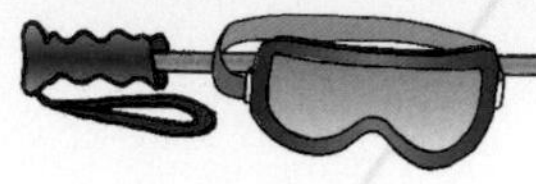

FAN PAGE

Which successful skier would you like to do an interview with?

___

What would you ask him or her?

___

___

___

Here you can collect autographs or paste photos of your idols!

. . . . 4 TRAINING – THE ROAD TO SUCCESS

Being able to ski the way the top athletes do would be awesome! You want to be fast, skillful and powerful. You want to ski the right line and achieve record times.

Surely you have noticed, during training or racing, that things don't always work as perfectly as you would like. Is your technique not quite up to par, are you still having trouble adjusting to the terrain or are your jumps still a little too hesitant? Moreover, you saw that the others ski pretty well, too, some even better than you. But not to worry!

No one is born a champion! The others started out just like you, and have gotten to where they are with lots of training.

But what can you do to become a good, and maybe even a top skier?

We want to help you train successfully for that with this book.

THE ROAD TO THE SKI SUMMIT

This book won't be able to replace your trainer. But it will explain why your trainer works with you on technique and form; why he says that you must improve your coordination, your endurance, your strength and flexibility.

You will learn to understand why it is necessary to do summer training in the gym in addition to snow training in winter.

You will recognize the importance of warming up and stretching before a race. And you will find out why it is that you sometimes think you aren't getting better, and why you don't do equally well every day.

Moreover, you will get suggestions on what you can do on your own, while practicing or outside of your regular practice sessions, to improve your performance and to independently monitor and evaluate your progress. The top skiers are able to do this. After many years of training and many races, they know exactly whether or not they are at their best, or what they need to work on to get even better.

Then the trainer is a good friend and advisor to them, but he sometimes needs to be strict when inner temptation says: "That's really exhausting today. I'm going to quit!"

Training actively and consciously

In skiing, anything you have to do actively and consciously to become a better skier is considered training.

Actively means that you have to do the training yourself. You don't get any better if your trainer tackles the run and knocks down the poles. Nor do you get better by putting the ski book under your pillow at night. It only works if you do it yourself, actively.

Consciously means that you understand the purpose and usefulness of the tasks your trainer gives you and carry them out independently. And maybe you can even think up and do some exercises of your own.

The opposite of conscious athletic training is mechanical training, which is done with racehorses and greyhounds. They only do what the animal trainer commands, without thinking about it.

So don't just do what you are told, but know why you are doing it! That is good for your success.

By the way, this isn't just true for sports but also for learning in school! If you know why you are doing something, you will enjoy it more and be more likely to persevere.

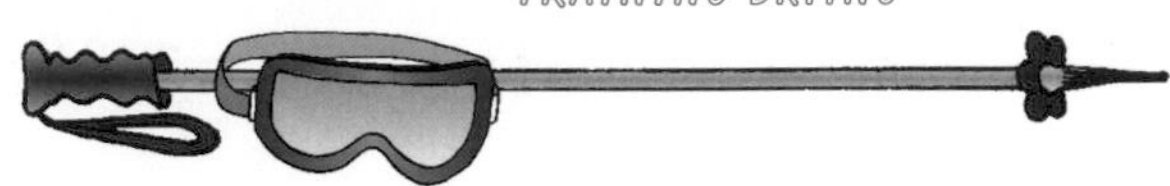

Since a skier must train many years to achieve very good performances, it makes sense to find out right from the start what it means to train properly, and to learn to train correctly. You will make faster progress than others in the same amount of training time, and in the end you will be more successful. And besides, training will be much more fun.

Training must be learned!

TRAINING RIGHT – BUT HOW?

A prerequisite to conscious training is being able to answer three questions:

 **What do I want to achieve?**

 **Why do I want to train?**

 **How can I train?**

What do I want to achieve? What are my training goals?

Clear goals are prerequisites to active and conscious training. If you don't have a goal, soon you will no longer enjoy training. Then you won't know why you are working so hard. A skier's most important goal is, of course, to have fun skiing. But, in the long term, it will only be fun if you continue to get a better feel for skis and snow, and are able to negotiate any terrain using a versatile skiing technique, even in varying snow conditions. You will get good results in racing and, compared to other skiers, will continue to perform better. Or would you be happy always being the worst one and losing?

Maybe your first goal is a really a big one: The Olympic competitions are being broadcast on television or you are watching a big World Cup race. All of the skiers are really concentrating and finding the right line. They arrive at the finish line in record time. Everyone cheers, amazed and thrilled. And you think: "I want to make it there, too!"

That's the way it should be!
But you have to remember that dreaming of victory is not the real thing. It will take a lot of sweat, and along with some small successes, there will also be many failures along the way.

Set some more immediate goals in addition to those big far-off ones. For instance, make a pledge to perfect your racing technique, to take that mandatory jump without jitters, and to cheat less often during fitness training.

Goals are what motivate every ambitious athlete!

It is fun to reach the goals you have set for yourself, and they give you incentive when something isn't working so well right away. But don't set unrealistic goals! Rather, choose those that are realistic and that you can reach in the near future.

Doesn't the trainer have to set the goals?

Now, you might think that this is the trainer's job. He could just tell you what you can and should achieve. He will do just that. He sets training goals for his athletes and puts together training plans for working with them. Of course, there are training programs and books for trainers.

But each skier knows himself best, knows his strengths and weaknesses. That is why he also knows best which goals to set for himself. And it is always good to set your own goals rather than have them "pressed" on you by someone else. Then they are your own goals and you are much more willing to do whatever it takes to fulfill them.

If you can tell your trainer exactly what you are having trouble with and what you would like to practice more in the near future, then he can respond to that by helping you train.

Imagine yourself in the following situations while you are working with a new trainer. How would you react?

1. *Your trainer asks you to go full speed off a rise in the terrain, even though you cannot see the landing spot on your approach, and you are not yet able to assess the course of the jump.*

2. *While doing speed control exercises, the trainer asks you to glide on flat terrain. In doing so you will have to negotiate several obstacles and then stop at the opposite uphill slope.*

Of course, the trainer and the athlete sometimes have different opinions. Occasionally, there is a discrepancy between the goals you have set for yourself and those the trainer envisions for you. It isn't easy for the trainer. If you feel his goals are too high, it means that he has a lot of confidence in you, but he might be asking too much of you. On the other hand, if you think his goals for you are not high enough, show him that you are capable of more.

Use the following table on page 32 to record your goals, including the date. Use the second column to write down the date you want to achieve your goal by. When you reach that goal, check it off and add the actual date you made it.

When the page is full, draw a new table and lay or paste it in the book. Or you can keep a "goal notebook" to use over a longer period of time.

What I want to achieve/date	Target date/ made it!
Be among the top five at the next practice run / 12.22	*(01.08)* *01.16* ✓
do 25 sit-ups	*(02.07)*

Overall goal and partial goals

At the last race, Bobby wasn't able to place. He did not meet the expectations of the trainer, his teammates, his parents or his own. But he doesn't know the cause, namely his poor racing technique. In his continued training, he has vowed to work specifically on his turning technique. That is his overall goal. Of course, he won't be able to concentrate on everything during the first few training sessions. That is why he has set partial goals, which will take him to his overall goal.

Here you can see what that means:

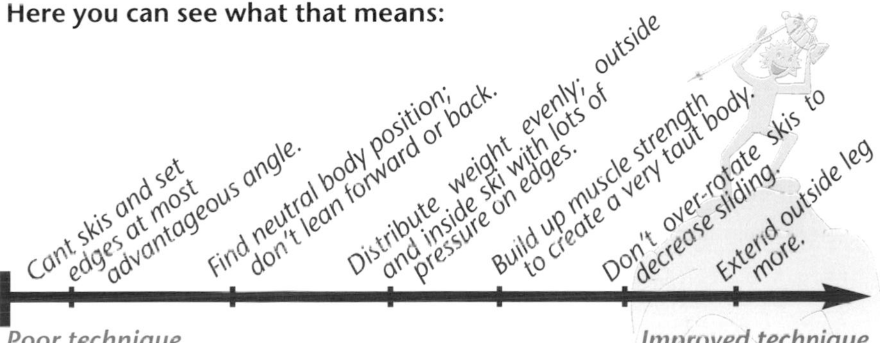

You also won't be able to instantly completely eliminate the occasional large sliding portions when making turns. Partial goals for improved turning as a training exercise might be, for instance:

- Stationary and mobile exercises with the bootlegs being pushed forward and inward.
- Changing the angle of the edges while moving at a diagonal.
- Executing turns uphill.
- Making turns on the outside leg, while lifting the inside leg.

This is how you can set partial goals for any of the techniques described in the book and then you can be happy when you make it.

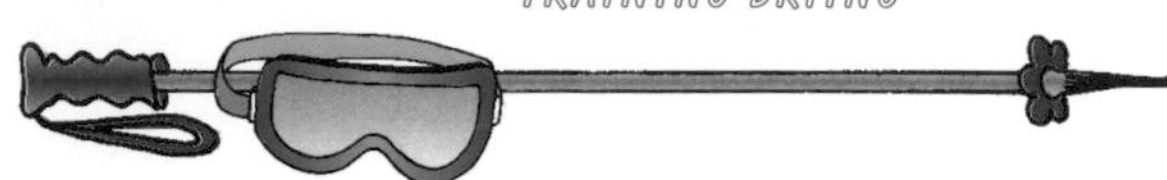

Why do I want to train in alpine skiing? What is the reason for my training? What are my motives?

The reason or *motive* for training is the "psychological motor" that initiates training. It decides whether or not you will go to training, whether you will fight or give in after a disappointment.

Going to training is never a problem when the weather is nice or you're bored. You want to get out in the fresh winter air to enjoy the white snow and the great runs. You will meet up with your friends and maybe your trainer has something exciting planned. But what happens when it rains, when there still isn't enough snow on the ground, the weather is yucky or there's a good show on television? Or on a beautiful summer day, when your friends are at the ice cream parlor or at the pool? How quickly do you get ready then?

If you really want to reach a partial goal and you know that the next training session is particularly important for the new season or for an upcoming race, the decision shouldn't be too difficult.

Review the reasons why you go to practice and work so hard. Decide whether a motive is very important, important or less important to you.

Put an X in the appropriate column of the table on page 35.

If you have any other reasons, add those on the two empty lines. You can also fill out this table again after one year. Maybe your motives will have changed by then.

I GO TO TRAINING AND TRY TO DO MY BEST ... ,

	Very important reason	Important reason	Not so important
because I love winter and snow.	☐	☐	☐
because I want to do something for my health.	☐	☐	☐
because I want to ski as well as my idol.	☐	☐	☐
because my parents want me to.	☐	☐	☐
because my friend is going, too.	☐	☐	☐
because I don't want to disappoint my trainer.	☐	☐	☐
because I want to gain recognition.	☐	☐	☐
because I don't have anything else to do.	☐	☐	☐
because I love the speed.	☐	☐	☐
because I want to be in the newspaper.	☐	☐	☐
because I want to make the national team.	☐	☐	☐
because I want to make money as a skiing professional some day.	☐	☐	☐
because I build my character through training.	☐	☐	☐
because skiing is just awesome.	☐	☐	☐
because ______________________________	☐	☐	☐
because ______________________________	☐	☐	☐

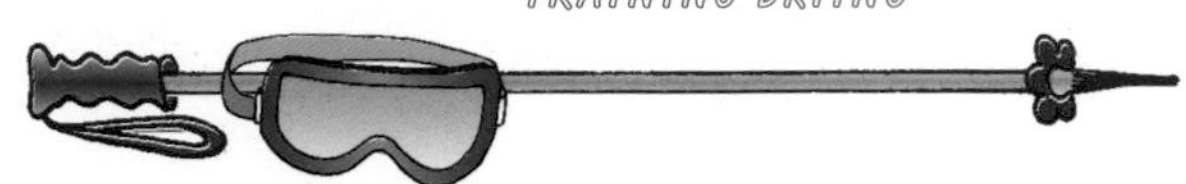

The trainer says to Max: "Ski this section as fast as you can!" Max tries his best and is pretty satisfied with his performance.

It's Tina's turn next. The trainer clocks a faster time for her. This annoys Max, even though he was pretty happy with his results. Now Max wants to race against Tina directly, because he can't accept his defeat (particularly by a girl)!

The final result doesn't really matter because, as you can imagine, Max now raced faster than he did before. Competing directly against Tina motivated him to ski faster.

A very important reason for doing all the training is knowing why you must do the individual exercises and how doing so helps you improve your performance.

Anything you do with interest you can do twice as well!

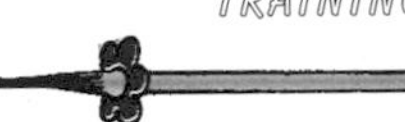

3 How can I train so I will reach my goals? How can I improve my performance through training?

The training effort that will lead to increased performance is known as training load. Just like each individual skier is different, so is the respective training load and the load required to improve performance. If an athlete does not exert himself sufficiently during training, he will not achieve an increase in performance, and if he exerts himself too much, it could cause exhaustion and lead to injuries due to a lack of concentration.

Unfortunately, there is no chart to tell the skier or trainer how high the load should be and can be. Every athlete has to help figure that out for himself. In the course of time, he will learn to "listen" to his own body and recognize when his load is high enough.

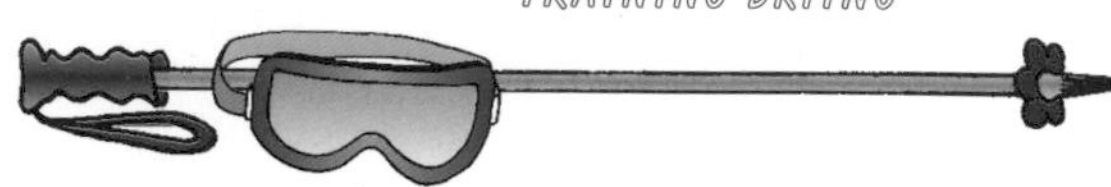

The correct training load will lead to an increase in performance because the body adjusts to the demand. The heart gets larger and more productive, the muscles grow stronger and you are able to concentrate over a longer period of time. After training regularly for some time, you will notice that exercises that used to get you out of breath before are no longer as strenuous. If you used to be totally exhausted after running for 15 minutes or doing two ski runs, you can now last longer.

Now it's time to increase the training load. Once again, your body will have to adjust and your performance will increase incrementally.

Many sports scientists and physicians have done research on which training method would be best suited for skiers to achieve maximum athletic performance and keep the body fit and healthy. Training at random usually doesn't produce the desired results. In fact, it can be damaging.

Surely you have noticed that your performance drops off when you don't train for a while. The first time you returned to training after a break the motion sequences and exercises seemed harder and your performance wasn't as good. So you had to start with a lesser training load than what you had ended your last training session with.

Training regularly is better than training irregularly!

Do you remember our example about reaching the summit? Laziness and irregular training disrupt performance development. You are thrown back a ways on the road to success. It's as though you are sliding back a bit on the path you already walked.

But often it isn't possible to train as diligently as you planned. There are times when you have to do more homework or you are on vacation with your parents. Maybe there isn't enough snow or the gym isn't always available.

If you set an athletic performance goal you should train regularly. Of course, that includes endurance sports, strength training and calisthenics. If you are not able to train due to illness or an injury, you definitely have to rest and get well. However, if you are not able to train because of vacation, school events, or other reasons, try to stay in shape anyway. Go jogging, do strength or balance exercises, stretch in your room or work on your flexibility. You can find specific exercises at various places in this book. It will make coming back after a break much easier.

Before you look at and read the following pages, answer these questions and write the answers on a piece of paper.

- ***What must a good skier be like?***
- ***What must a successful skier be able to do?***
- ***What does his performance depend on?***

____

____

____

WHAT IT TAKES TO BE A GOOD SKIER

Surely you thought of some good answers to our questions on page 39. There is much a good skier must know, have, and be able to do. This chart is an attempt to illustrate all the things that factor into a skier's performance and what kind of training is necessary. It is impossible to view the individual factors independent of each other. That is why the circles in the illustration overlap. Since everything is affected by mental abilities, the circle encloses everything. In addition, there are important outside influences, illustrated by the outer arrows.

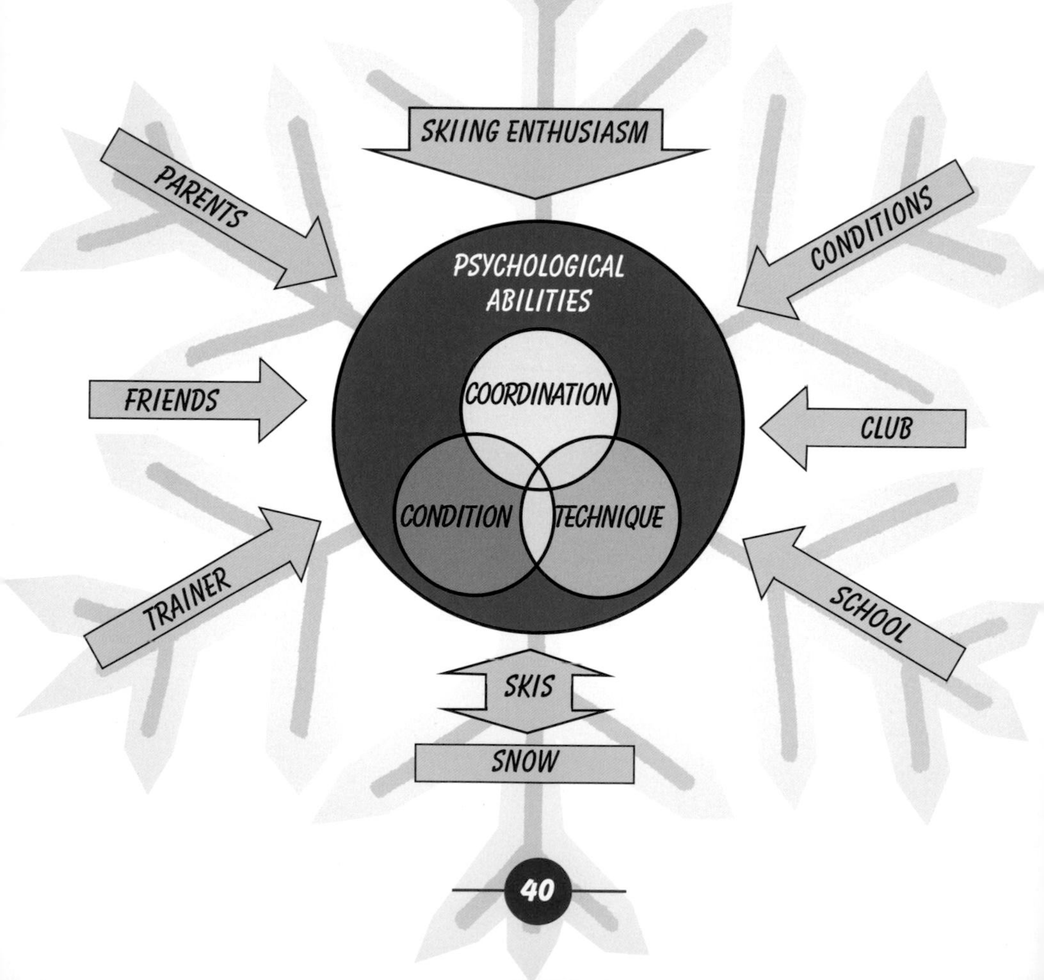

SKIING ENTHUSIASM
PARENTS
CONDITIONS
PSYCHOLOGICAL ABILITIES
FRIENDS
COORDINATION
CLUB
CONDITION
TECHNIQUE
TRAINER
SCHOOL
SKIS
SNOW

Technique refers to the special movements in skiing. These include gliding, canting (setting an edge), weight shifting and turning. A good start and a skillful jump are also important.

When a skier has plenty of endurance and strength, is quick and flexible, he is said to have good **condition**. Skiing a run, running a slalom or, of course, an entire competition requires lots of strength and stamina. You have to stay totally fit and focused the entire time.

While you are moving fast, you are constantly alternating between putting down weight, releasing weight, turning, jumping, etc. You have to continuously readjust to the conditions of the terrain, find your center of gravity over your skis and keep adjusting the movements of your legs, arms and body. **Coordination** is very important for that.

The **psychological abilities** determine how confident, competitive or anxious you are, and whether a mistake at a gate or a messed up run will discourage you, or spur you on to try all the harder.

Our chart also shows arrows for **parents, friends, trainer, conditions, club and school**. (You could certainly add more to the list.) All of these are external influences, which impact the skier's performance. Whether or not your parents support your training is very important. How well you get along with your trainer and your training buddies is also relevant. And one can't deny the motivating force of blue sky, sunshine and fresh glittering snow. It is difficult to focus when you have problems at school or stress at home. It makes a difference whether lots of spectators are cheering, the sun is shining and you like your new ski outfit, or whether you are not being noticed, the run is slushy, your ski boots pinch and the old skis won't glide. And without the necessary **skiing enthusiasm**, you likely won't achieve your top performance.

All of the factors combined bring success

Only with good conditioning will you ever become a super long distance runner or a focused chess player; you need good technique to become a great juggler or excellent coordination to be a celebrated acrobat. But an alpine racer needs it all. And if our control system, the psyche, fails, everything can go topsy-turvy, just like a computer without its software. But assembling all of the components at once is very difficult. That is why you have to train everything step by step to become a successful skier.

What does that mean for your training?

Of course, your condition, coordination, technique and a feel for racing are best improved with training. Those who spend a lot of time on the runs definitely have the best chance at making progress. But if you sense particular weaknesses in one area, additional training becomes necessary. In the following chapters, we will explain the individual factors more thoroughly and talk about training methods. We will make suggestions for exercises you can do at home, for self-monitoring and evaluating your performance. Also, discuss everything with your trainer. He knows the ropes.

........5 MENTAL ABILITIES

Why is it that humans can feel joy and sadness, that they can fall in love or hate someone? Why are humans able to think, remember and dream?

People have always wanted to know what goes on inside their bodies. No one had an explanation, so they called the whole thing the soul. The famous physician Rudolf Virchow (1821 – 1902) once asked his students to find the soul in the human body. But what they found in the corpses they dissected were the brain, the heart, the lungs, the liver, and all of the other organs. But they did not find a soul.

Of course, they could not have found it, because our ability to perceive and imagine, to think and decide, and to feel and want are results of our brain's activity. The science that deals with this is called *psychology*, and the old term soul was replaced with the word *psyche*.

Thus, mental or *psychological abilities* refers to the skier's ability to handle joy, anger, rage, excitement, competitiveness, fear, and many other feelings, and the ability to advantageously and successfully apply them in training and during competitions. In psychology, research is also done on how the thinking process works and how our muscles receive commands. We imagine our brain as a computer that controls everything. While you ski your "computer" is working at high capacity, which is why it needs to be well prepared.

WHAT DOES OUR "COMPUTER" LOOK LIKE ON THE INSIDE?

We don't want to make this a technical lecture. Besides, the brain as a topic is far too complicated and extensive to describe in a short chapter. But some people really believe that sports are strictly about muscles. They don't realize that the muscles' impulses come from the brain and that every complex athletic movement and action is controlled by nerve connections in the brain.

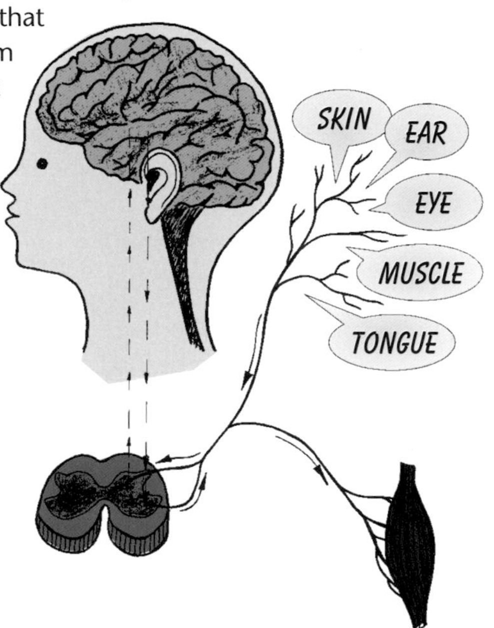

To make sure you understand the importance of the brain in skiing, we definitely cannot leave a chapter like this one out of a training book.

The path of perception – circuit – brain – muscle

In the illustration, you can see a simplified version of how the process works. You receive lots of information via receptors located in our sensory organs. You can see, hear, taste and feel things.

Nerve tracts then carry this information to the brain. On the way to the brain, the information first arrives at a circuit. In our drawing, it is a piece of bone marrow located in the spinal column. The brain sends an "order" to the respective muscle, telling it what task to perform.

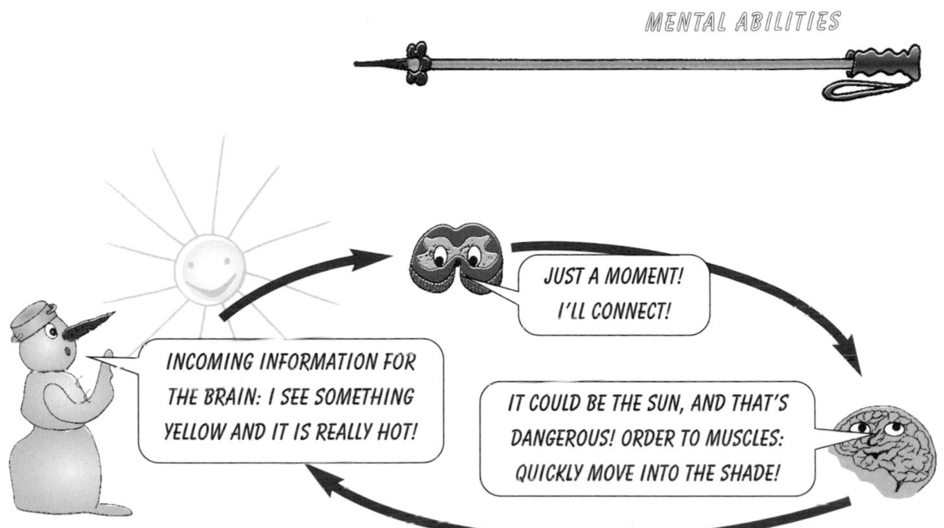

Conscious reaction

Most impulses and information gathered through our senses are transmitted from the circuits to the appropriate areas of the brain. After a review of the incoming impulses, they are compared to experiences and mentally processed. Orders for executing conscious actions travel on nerve tracts from the cerebral cortex to the muscles via the spinal marrow (that was the circuit).

An example:

- *Incoming impulse:*
  You are skiing very fast and see a sharp turn coming up.
- *Compare with experiences:*
  You know you will be carried out of the turn if you don't apply your edges enough and don't exert enough strength.
- *Mental preparation:*
  Increase body tension, heavy edging, tighten muscles, use torso to create counter force ...

Pretty difficult! But not to worry! Most of this stuff develops when you train properly and have gathered a few experiences.

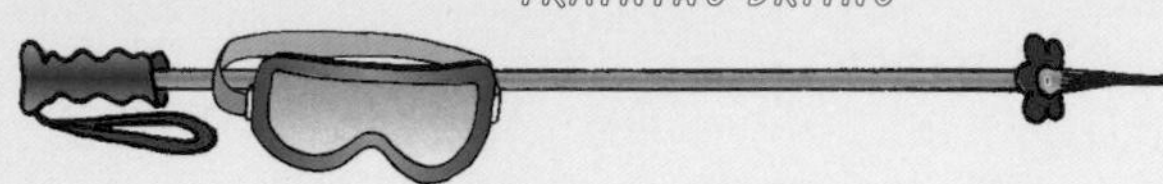

1 *Building a snowman: find 11 differences!*

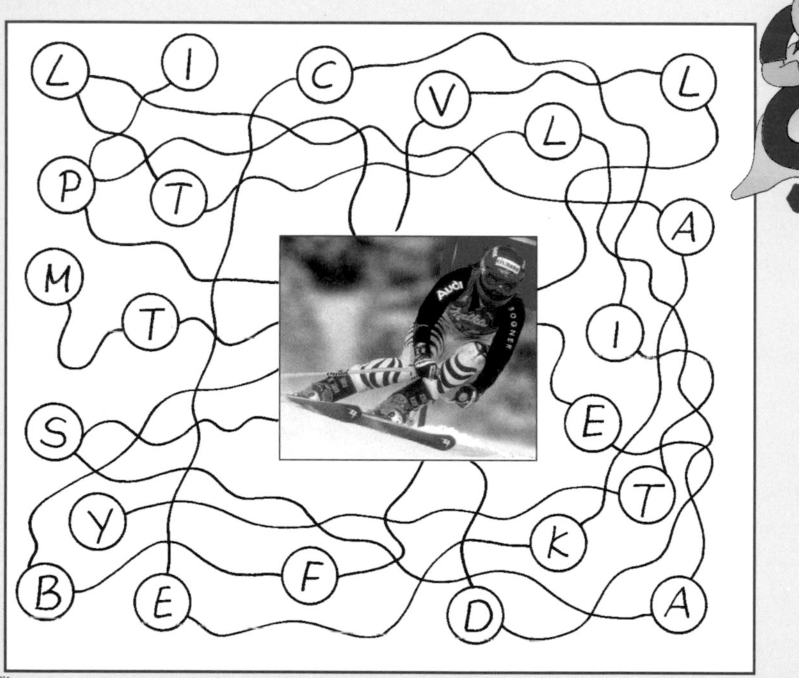

2 *A city that was once host to the Olympic games is hidden here! You will figure out the name of the city, if you can find the correct beginning of the track and continue to follow the 12 letters.*

Reflexes

Are you familiar with the following situation? You accidentally touch a hot stove top and quickly pull your hand away, or you are blinded by bright light and squeeze your eyes shut, or you slip on a slick surface and flail your arms to keep from falling down. In these situations, your muscles react automatically without your having to think about what to do. This type of reaction is called a reflex. Since you don't have to first think about what to do, the information also does not have to be forwarded to the brain. The impulse goes from the circuit straight to the muscle.

In skiing, this becomes apparent, for instance, if you suddenly start to slide or thread. You have to react quickly and don't have a lot of time to think. Thus, the skier can safely be in control of any situation.

Practicing in various snow and surface conditions will help you react quickly. You gather experiences and develop reflexes. You have probably guessed by now how important it is to know a lot about your sport. A skier can decide much faster what a certain impulse means and what the appropriate response would be if he is well prepared and doesn't have to spend a lot of time thinking about it.

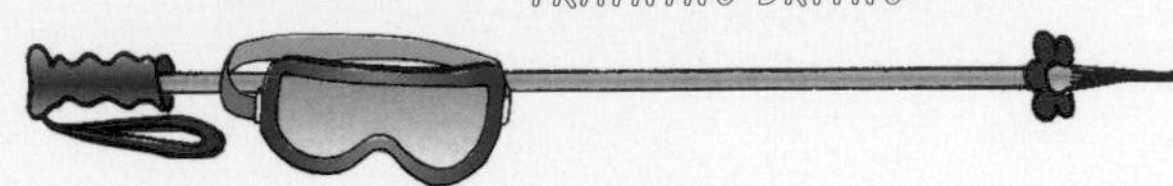

REACTION EXERCISES

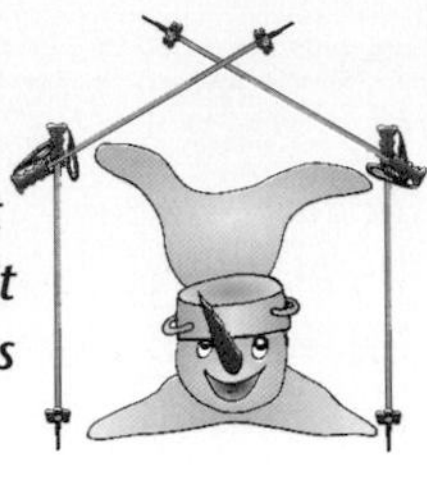

These exercises will help you recognize the right moment and then react as quick as lightning. Anyone who thinks it would be fun is the perfect practice partner. That includes friends, parents, grandparents, siblings, etc.

One partner places a coin or some other small object in his open palm. You hold your hand under his and try to find the right moment to suddenly take the coin from him. Your partner must quickly close his hand or pull it away.

You're allowed to take turns.

Your partner positions himself as shown in the illustration. The hands are approximately eight inches apart. You try to move your hand through the gap between his hands. He has to clap his hands together to catch you.

Try to move your hand at varying speeds to trick or outsmart your partner.

Try the following trick:
Start out really fast and then stop just before you get to his hands. Of course, he'll clap his hands together. When he opens them again, move your hand through nice and slow.

DEXTERITY GAMES

Before practice or in the lunch line at school, everyone is standing around looking bored. How about some dexterity games for those moments? They're fun and make the time pass faster. Just be careful not to get in other people's way.

Touching the knee
Stand across from your partner and try to touch each other's knee. At the same time, you have to protect your own knee by dodging your partner's hand. You can even form teams.

Stepping on toes
Once again, stand across from your partner. Now try to step on each other's toes. Be careful not to let your own toes get stepped on.

Please remember: This is about dexterity and not about hurting your partner!

Shadow
One partner continuously stays at the left or right side of the other partner, who tries to ditch him by walking, running or turning. (Don't spin in circles.) Who can be a shadow the longest without getting ditched?

Catching the glove
Your partner holds a ski glove or a similar object in his hand. You stand in front of him. He will suddenly let go of the object and you have to try to quickly catch it before it hits the ground. Take turns!

TACTICS

You are totally prepared, have trained well and regularly and your skis are in prime condition. Now you just hope you're lucky and the snow is right for you and the course is to your liking. Was that everything? Is there nothing left for you to do? Of course, there is more to do. The athlete thinks about the preparation process, chooses the right material, reviews the course and plans his race. These are tactics.

You use tactics to apply your skiing skills in the best way possible, so you can be as fast as possible.

Reviewing the course

The course is not a regulation playing field that you could train on and navigate with your eyes closed. A close inspection of the course is definitely part of preparing for a race. You look at the course, preferably with your trainer or your teammates. You find the best line to follow, look for peculiarities and treacherous places, and discuss the race progression.

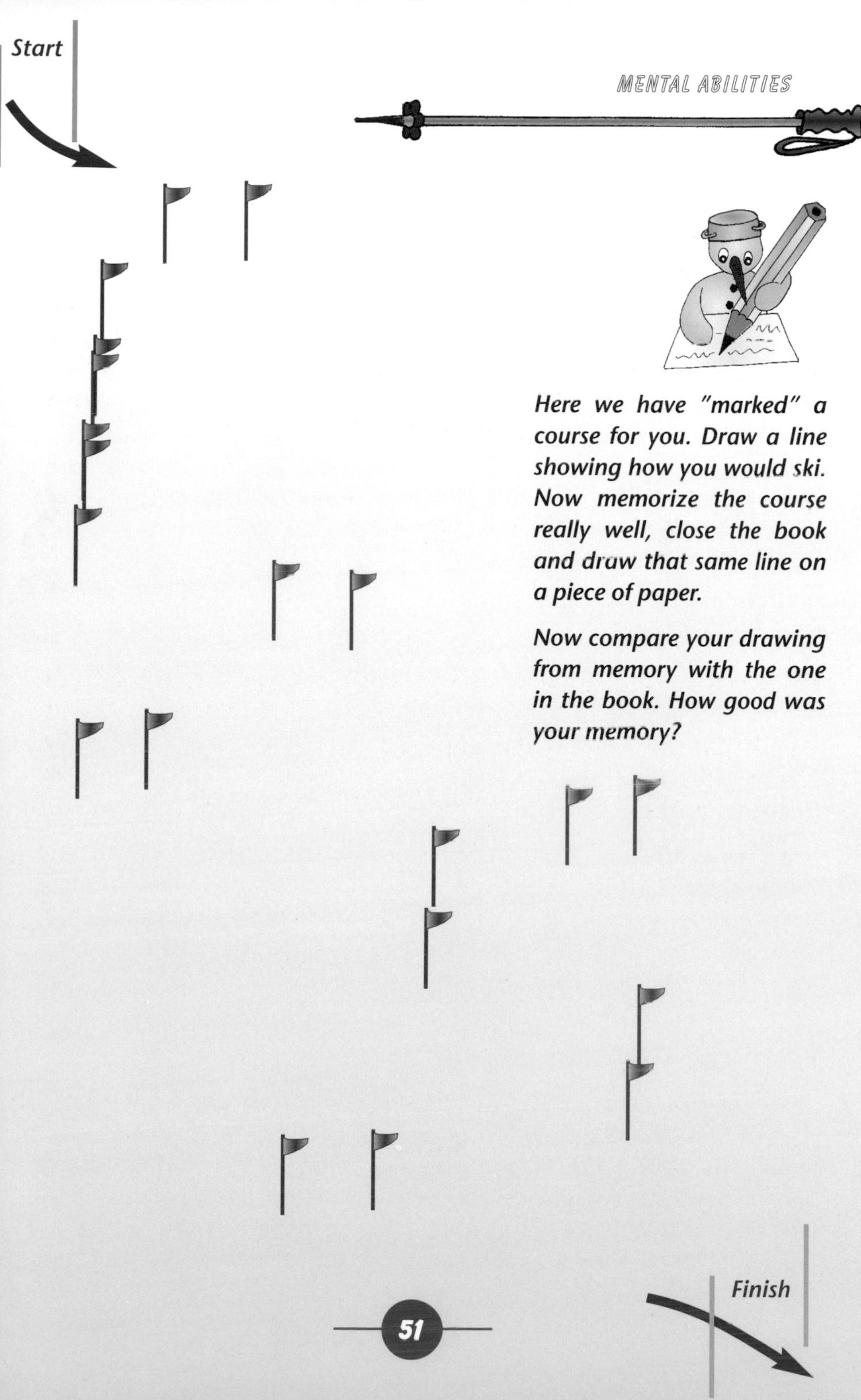

Here we have "marked" a course for you. Draw a line showing how you would ski. Now memorize the course really well, close the book and draw that same line on a piece of paper.

Now compare your drawing from memory with the one in the book. How good was your memory?

YOUR MENTAL STATE IMPACTS YOUR PERFORMANCE

You are training hard to prepare for a race. You continue to work on your condition and fine-tune your technique. You get tips, correct mistakes and practice until it works. Now you're super-well prepared and really just need to do everything the way you do it in training. But what's this? You are trembling with anxiety, are afraid you'll fail or something will go wrong. You can barely concentrate on the race. Are you now hopelessly at the mercy of your emotions and your trembling legs, or can the psyche also be trained? Well, we want to reassure you that there is something you can do about that!

First of all, it is very important to know what is going on inside you. If you know the causes, you are better able to adjust and prepare yourself for such situations.

Tension and nervousness

Being nervous before a competition is normal and important. No athlete will be successful if he stays totally cool and laid-back. The inner tension helps you to perform at your best. But too much anxiety can be damaging. You may have trouble concentrating, may be tense and, most importantly, you may make dangerous mistakes.

Fear

There are various reasons why an alpine skier might be afraid. Sometimes it is fear of skiing poorly and failing. It might be the speed or that anxious feeling on a hard run. Turns and jumps can also appear very complicated and impossible at first glance. Maybe you recently took a painful fall. A little respect is quite useful. It makes you more serious and attentive. Besides, a fearful skier is unsure and lacks the necessary bite. You can

combat this negative feeling in training in conversations with your trainer, your parents or friends. Relaxation exercises are also often helpful.

Anger

You can be angry about many things – your trainer, your parents, your friend, a competitor, school, etc. Maybe that run isn't going as well, in training or at competition, as you had planned. Do you sometimes get angry at your "terrible skis?" You have to learn to handle feelings of aggression. Don't let your anger out on your trainer or your training buddies. When you feel anger in your belly, try to channel that feeling into approaching your task with more focus and determination. Be resolute – but not unfair! Stay calm and turn it into an incentive.

Giving yourself a little pep talk can often help you calm down, give you courage and spur you on.

STAY CALM! AFTER ALL, YOU TRAINED REALLY HARD!

TODAY I WILL WIN!

MY PARENTS WILL BE AMAZED!

I'M STRONGEST IN THE FINISH!

DON'T LOSE YOUR COOL!

THAT MISTAKE IS AGGRAVATING, BUT IT'S NOT OVER TILL IT'S OVER!

TODAY IS MY DAY!

Overcoming fear

In extreme situations, an alpine ski racer has to face his fear and take it to the limit. He is also supposed to keep up in training, increase his performance and, if necessary, just clench his teeth and bear it. Always look for new challenges and always be ready to try something new. You will continue to reach your limits and learn to push past them to a reasonable degree.

Such challenges could be:

Fear of moving at high speed.
("I will lose control, I'm going too fast! Help, I'm going to fall!")

Physical limitations in training
("I can't do it anymore, it's too exhausting! I have to quit. My entire body aches!")

Fear of new things
("The way I did it in the past always worked so well! I bet, with this new technique I'll do worse again!")

Conflict with trainer or sports buddies
("Nobody understands me! Nobody likes me!")

- ***Overcome your fear and you'll be proud of yourself later.***
- ***In sports, willpower will strengthen you and help you cope with problems at school and in other areas of your life.***
- ***If you're not sure how to handle your problems, get some advice. Talk to your parents, trainer, friends or your doctor.***

Attention span and concentration

Whether the sun is just coming out from behind the clouds, the rescue helicopter is landing in an adjacent valley or your biggest competitor has new equipment, don't get distracted! Before a race, the athlete has to fully concentrate on his movements and on the course. Thoughts about personal problems or your competitors, or fear of possible mistakes or poor results only distract you. School problems or thinking about what to wear to the next party also must be put aside while training or during a competition. The more difficult the task, the more you need to concentrate. During the race everything happens very quickly. Just a brief moment of inattention and you may lose precious seconds.

Tips to improve your attention span

To pay attention, you have to want to!
If you don't really feel like concentrating on your homework, every little thing will distract you. You think about what your friends might be doing right now, you watch a bird fly past the window and pay attention to every noise in the house. Before you concentrate, tell yourself why you are doing it and what it is good for.

Let no one and nothing distract you!
Compare yourself to a spotlight that is aimed at a single spot. Only this spot is lit, everything else stays dark. Concentrate on the run. Just taking a peek to see what's going on at the edge of the run can cause mistakes. Even thinking about what would happen if you did something wrong is distracting, and you are no longer focused on the race.

Take concentration breaks!
Your ability to concentrate is not endless. Every human being must rest and gather strength.

Do you have enough imagination?

There once was a little hat-bug in love, walking along on a ribbon to get to his sweetheart. Will he make it or will he arrive on the back of the ribbon?

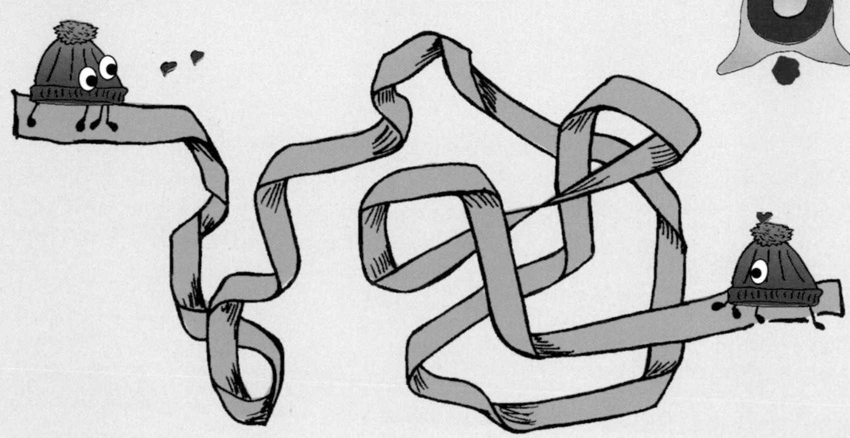

How observant are you?

Closely look at the photo on page 9 for ten seconds. (Count to 10!) Then come back to this page and try to answer the following questions from memory.

1 *How many skiers are shown on the photo?* ....

2 *Are there one or two athletes on the left side?* ....

3 *Can you see blue ski?* ....

4 *What color are the athletes' sleeves?* ....

5 *Which ski marker can be seen in the background?*

....

SELF-CONFIDENCE

Some people say that self-confidence is half the battle! Of course, it isn't that simple, but there is some truth to that saying. Someone who approaches a task with self-confidence, joy and pep, who believes in himself and his ability, certainly has a better chance at success than the one who is anxious and full of self-doubt.

But don't get cocky and start making mistakes because you are too self-confident!

Which of the following qualities and attitudes are useful to an alpine racer, and which ones are more of a hindrance? Cross out the ones you don't want to have too much of.

Self-confidence – enjoys skiing – self-doubt – blind anger – risk taker – impatience – laid back – fear of making mistakes – ambition – competitiveness – confidence in one's ability – pessimism – bad mood – feeling in good form – alertness – concentration.

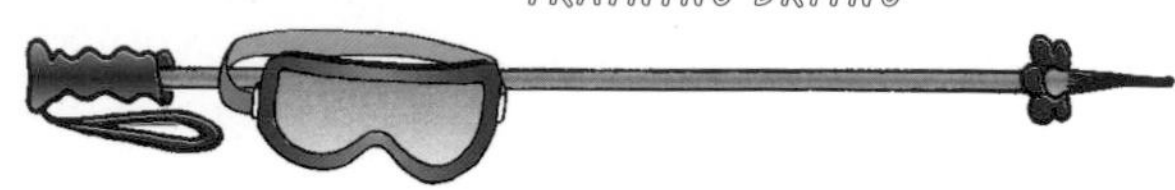

Even the best athlete loses sometimes

When you're too slow and can't find the right line, or you're making technical mistakes or even take a fall, you're asking yourself what went wrong. Maybe the course was too difficult and the competitors were older than you. They have been training longer and therefore are stronger. Maybe snow conditions weren't favorable and your skis weren't properly tuned. Don't be angry but keep training. If you're good, next time will be better. Be happy about doing your personal best.

But if you think you should have done better, then think about the reasons and causes.

This chart for recording the reasons for your poor performances will help you improve.

When was I not satisfied with my performance?	*What were the reasons?*	*What do I want to work on in the near future?*
December 3 / Race at Hidden Valley	*Not many mistakes but went too slow.*	*Ski more aggressively and more gutsy.*
January 22 / Competition in Crested Butte	*Approached the third gate and fell.*	*Pay more attention and concentrate while skiing.*

SELF-IMPOSED PRESSURE BUILDS MENTAL STRENGTH

What do you think when you read the story about Julie? Does it sound familiar?

Julie was looking forward to the race. She told everyone how well things were going in training and that the trainer had registered her for the next race. She prepared really well. She packed her bag the night before and checked everything off her list. Now it's just early to bed and plenty of sleep for the big day! But then she misses a gate in the middle section of the course and is disqualified. Everyone is surprised and wonders what's going on with Julie today.

What happened to Julie is something that can happen even to successful athletes at important races.

The pressure was just too much; she was too anxious and couldn't give her usual performance. It isn't the end of a career, but it is very annoying!

You should understand why such a situation occurs and what you can do about it.

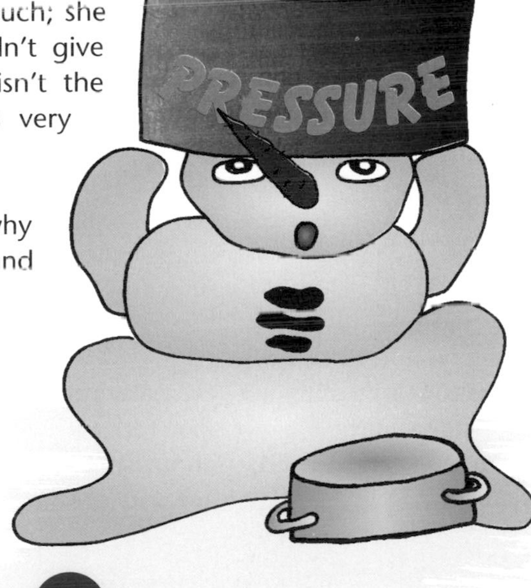

Pressure has to do with expectations

First of all there are external expectations.

They come from your parents, your trainer and your friends. They all expect you to perform well.

And then there are your personal expectations. You want to achieve the goals you set for yourself.

Sometimes performance pressure gets to be too much. You are afraid that you won't be able to meet the high expectations of others or your own. And that's stressful!

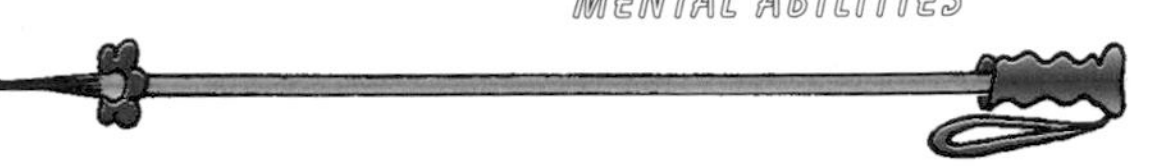

How to deal with pressure

Use your training sessions during the week to prepare for the race. Train diligently and stay focused. Mentally prepare yourself for the demands that await you, then nothing that happens will surprise you.

Get everything ready the night before, check your equipment, go to bed early, have a good breakfast and leave the house on time.

Leave behind all problems that have nothing to do with the race. Imagine that no outside problems can touch you once you're on the course. Concentrate only on your movements and the course.

You choose the pressure yourself. You set the goals and decide what you want to achieve. Of course, you could set easier-to-reach goals, thereby avoiding the pressure, by choosing to ski slower, not wanting to win anyway or not even starting at all. Set your goals high but be realistic. A little pressure is necessary. It is fun and spurs you on.

Pressure shapes your character! You will only be strong if you can handle situations with pressure. Each time you will be able to handle more pressure. Someone who already avoids any pressure in the preparation phase will become "soft" and will always stay below his potential. Someone who overcomes his weaker self strengthens his character.

Observe successful athletes as they relax and concentrate before a race, at the start and during breaks. How do they handle mistakes, successes and defeats?

Try to imitate them and find out what feels right for you. Practice these actions and carry them out often. Traits you develop in skiing will also be helpful in other areas of your life.

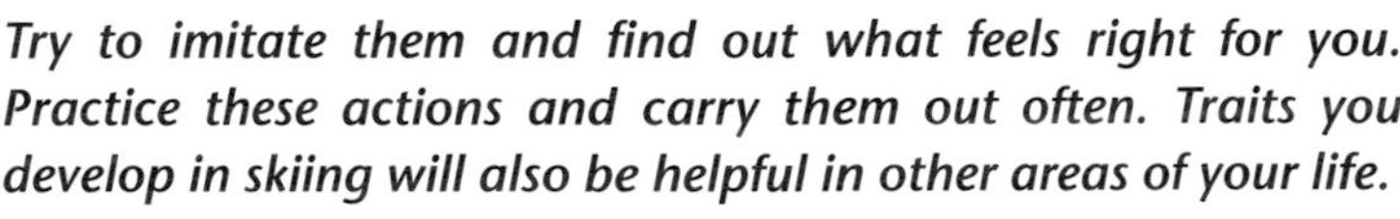

TEST

How would you react in the following situations?

1. Situation: You don't feel like going to training.

A. You stay home because no one should do anything they don't want to do. 1

B. You go to training without any enthusiasm because you don't want to disappoint your parents. 2

C. You go to training like you always do because if you miss it, you'll get worse again. Maybe you'll feel like training once you're on your skis. 3

2. Situation: The trainer repeatedly criticizes your turning technique.

A. It's annoying that it still isn't working properly. But right now it's time to practice setting an edge correctly. 2

B. He shouldn't always be so picky. It's not a beauty contest. One more word and you'll leave! 1

C. It's good that the trainer is always watching. It will keep you from picking up certain mistakes. 3

3. Situation: The course looks pretty difficult.

A. You are totally focused, breathing calmly, and are mentally reviewing the course once more. 3

B. You think you'll easily make it. You take one more look to see if all of your relatives are there and wave to them. 2

C. You're afraid you'll "mess the whole thing up." It's already predestined that you'll fall on approach. Besides, you don't have a chance against the others. 1

4. Situation: Last week, the trainer told you that Tom will take your place at the next race.

A. You think that's too bad; maybe you just weren't good enough. 2
B. You're upset because you're at least as good as Tom. Hopefully he won't do well and you can say, "I would have been faster!" 1
C. You help and support Tom in everything he needs. You work hard in training so next time you'll be asked to go again. 3

5. Situation: You are about to approach the final gate when you lose your rhythm.

A. That was bound to happen. The set-up of those gates was too complicated. 1
B. That can happen. Now concentrate on the next turn. 3
C. Now just get through it without embarrassing yourself too much. 2

6. Situation: You observe another racer secretly tampering with the favorite's racing skis.

A. You confront him and demand that he immediately correct the situation. 3
B. You sit back and wait. It's not your problem; no need to get involved in everything. 2
C. Great idea! If the favorite is eliminated, you have a good chance at winning. 1

Add up your points! You will find your score in the solutions section.

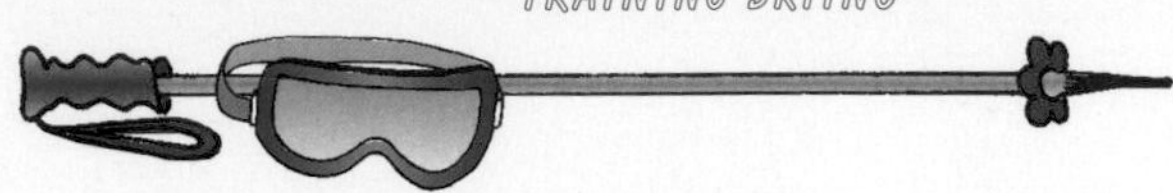

RELAXATION EXERCISES

To relax, find a quiet place where no one will disturb you. Stretch out, sit down or lean against the wall and close your eyes. The most important part is breathing correctly.

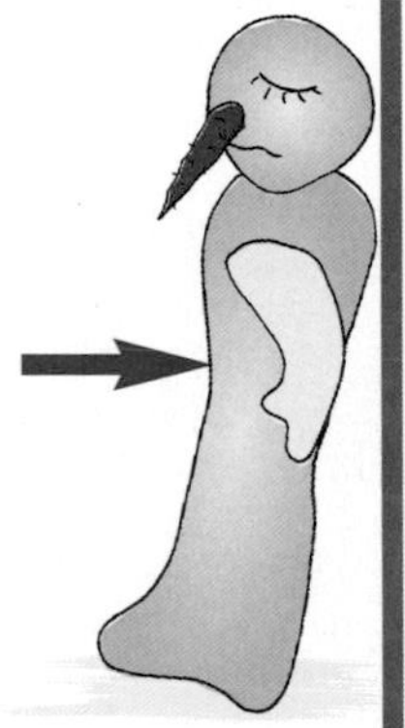

Exhale slowly and quietly, letting your stomach flatten.

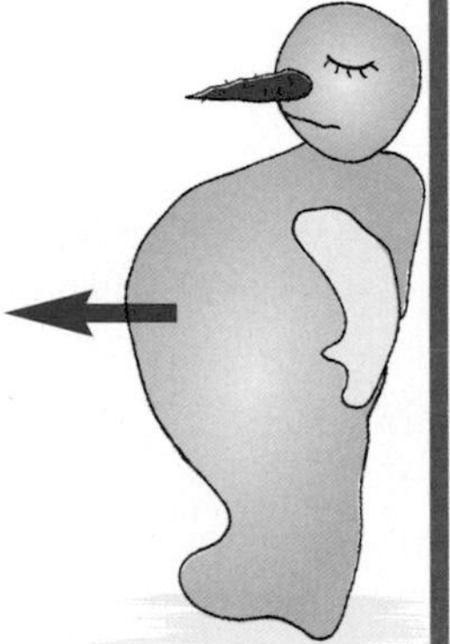

Inhale deeply, making your stomach nice and round.

The following exercises will stretch muscles and tendons. You'll feel a slight pulling. It feels good but shouldn't hurt. Hold the position as long as you can. No bouncing! Don't forget to breathe deeply as you do these exercises! You can find additional exercises in yoga books.

Make yourself really small like a little package.

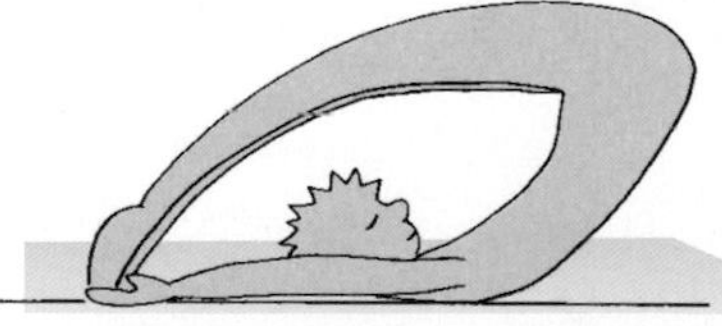

Lie on your back and fold your legs over your head.

From a kneeling position, sit back on your heels and flatten out your torso, making it really long.

. . . . 6 CONDITIONING

Max visits the doctor because he thinks there is something wrong with his body. "I don't know what's wrong with me. Yesterday we all practiced on a slalom run. I was totally exhausted and could barely stand when I got to the finish. Besides that, my thighs were hurting and my arms were cramping!"

"You probably didn't train enough!"

"I did! I go to training three times a week. I practice setting edges correctly and shifting my weight."

"What else do you practice?"

"What do you mean? I'm skiing the whole time!"

What will the doctor tell Max? Of course, his training is too one-sided. He forgot about fitness training and body conditioning. He has no endurance or strength, and his joints are not flexible. His body can't sustain intense downhill ski training with several test runs.

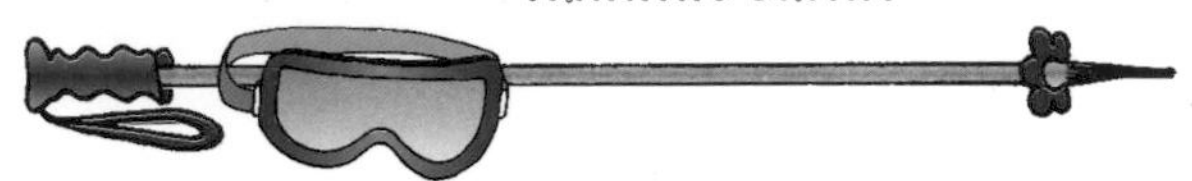

WHAT CONDITIONING MEANS

In sports, the term *conditioning* refers primarily to physical abilities. Your condition determines how much endurance you have, how fast and how strong you are, and how much physical strain you can handle. You can tell whether or not you are in good condition by how winded you get after a short race, how long you can endure athletic strain without all of your limbs aching, or how quickly you get tired.

You can achieve good condition by training regularly on the runs. But you can also get in shape or improve it by doing a variety of sports. And, of course, by participating in school sports.

S	W	I	M	M	I	N	G	T	M	O	P	L	X	H
H	F	C	R	O	S	S	C	O	U	N	T	R	Y	G
I	G	E	L	R	U	I	M	W	S	I	N	N	E	T
K	N	S	F	E	S	N	O	T	N	I	M	D	A	B
I	I	K	F	P	T	G	N	I	L	C	Y	C	I	B
N	E	A	X	E	R	E	C	C	O	S	Z	W	B	U
G	O	T	V	L	X	S	N	I	U	K	P	U	T	E
X	N	I	H	L	Z	R	Y	R	T	N	C	P	M	W
J	A	N	R	I	G	K	F	M	I	W	Z	Q	N	X
H	C	G	M	N	W	I	L	L	A	B	D	N	A	H
J	U	D	O	G	N	J	O	G	G	I	N	G	B	X
N	V	S	O	G	Y	M	N	A	S	T	I	C	S	L
T	Y	B	Y	W	L	L	A	B	Y	E	L	L	O	V
B	I	G	N	I	T	A	K	S	E	N	I	L	N	I

Some sports are for individuals while others can only be played in teams. In addition there are typical summer and winter sports. We have hidden 17 of these horizontally, vertically or diagonally, forward and backward in this crossword puzzle. Can you find them?

CONDITIONAL ABILITIES

We will now take a closer look at the types of conditional or physical abilities an alpine skier needs to be in all-around good shape. These include:

Endurance

Endurance is the performance prerequisite required for enduring physical strain over an extended period of time. That includes not getting tired too quickly during strenuous training, during a long day of competing or, for instance, on long trips to racing locations. Your body should also be able to recover quickly after a big exertion. This is called *regenerating*. People with good endurance are physically fit, recover more quickly after training or competing, and are able to concentrate longer. An alpine skier needs good endurance so that on competition day he is able to complete all of his races at the highest speed possible without being slowed down by exhaustion. He maintains good form and makes powerful turns all the way to the finish. That requires *strength endurance*.

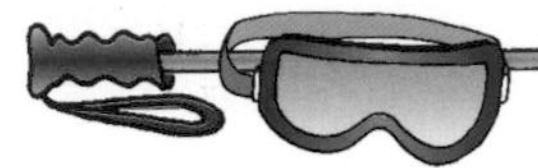

How can you train for endurance?

The best and most important training is, of course, practicing racing on the slopes in snow. But maybe you don't often have the opportunity or the weather conditions aren't right. There is a variety of suitable sports, like running, inline-skating, bicycling, swimming, cross-country skiing. Sports that require lots of running, like handball, soccer, field hockey, tennis, etc., provide great endurance training.

Speed

Speed is needed to execute a movement with the fastest possible acceleration and speed. You need *speed of movement*, which is a quick technique conversion, and *speed of reaction*, reacting with lightning speed in a new situation.

How can you train for speed?

Once again, the rule applies: The best speed training is on your skis. Therefore, you should not engage in slow motion training, but as soon as you have mastered the motion sequence practice at full speed.

Off the slopes, any ballgame in which you have to move fast and react very quickly is just right. But, as we already mentioned in the chapter "Mental Abilities," you can also train and improve your speed by doing sprints (even on a bicycle), jumping rope fast, or by playing other reaction games.

Strength

If you want to move something heavy, you need strength for lifting, thrusting, pulling or pushing weights. You also need strength to hold your body or body parts in a certain position, to move very quickly or to slow down movement.

An alpine skier makes powerful turns, sets edges, and has to hold the optimum line, even in difficult snow conditions. In doing so, you keep your body taut, often skiing in a tucked position while your arms and knees remain flexed. Powerful arm-pole work helps with balance, supports your turns, and knocks the slalom poles out of the way through narrow gates.

How can you train for strength?

Surely you have seen the many apparatuses fitness studios have for athletes to steel their muscles with. Actually, you don't really need those elaborate "strength machines," but with simple weights and your own body weight, you can get yourself in shape. Again, we have included various exercises in this book.

Don't forget to warm up and stretch so you don't injure yourself while doing the strength exercises.

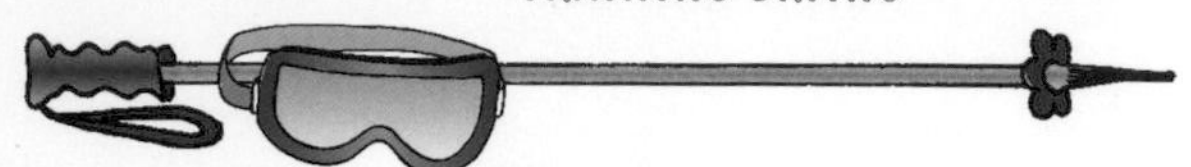

EXERCISES WITH A RUBBER BAND

This simple but versatile piece of equipment has proven valuable to many athletes working on strength training. This rubber band is approximately four feet long and five inches wide, is inexpensive and takes up very little space. It fits in any bag. It is available under various names from different manufacturers.

Here are a few exercise examples. Don't forget to warm up!

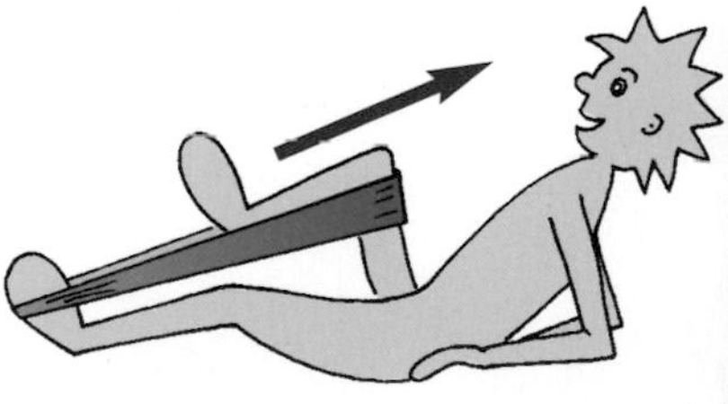

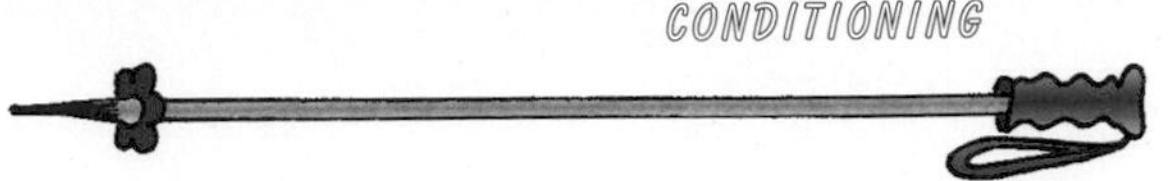

JUMPING EXERCISES

Surely we don't need to tell you how important take-off power is for an alpine skier. Here are a few exercises you can use to improve your take-off strength.

High jumps

Stand flat on your feet against a wall. Reach up with one arm as high as you can and mark that spot with tape or chalk.

Pushing off with both legs, jump as high as you can (maximum height). Mark the height of your jump at the highest point you were able to reach with your hand. If you're practicing by yourself, hold a piece of chalk in your hand and mark as you jump. (Watch the good wallpaper in the living room or the neighbor's wall!) The difference between reaching height and jumping height is your jumping performance.

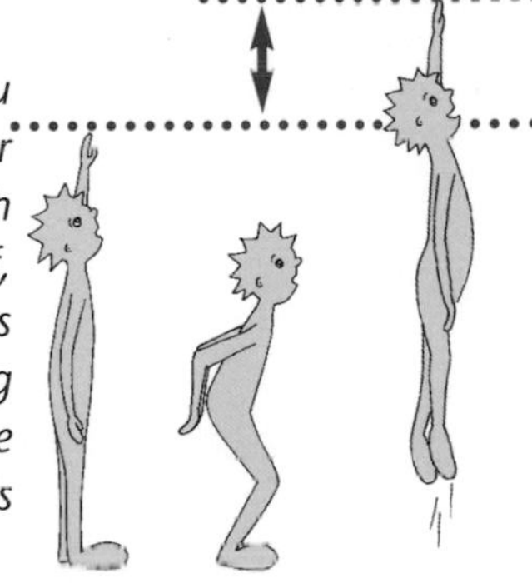

Stair jumping

In your starting position, you face the stairs, feet together, arms slightly bent at your sides. Now jump up the stairs as fast as you can. Careful! Don't trip! The arms support the jump and help keep your balance. This exercise is about being fast and light-footed.

Two-legged jumps

This jumping exercise improves the explosive power of leg and hip muscles, but also to some extent the arm and shoulder musculature. While standing with your knees slightly bent, swing your arms to gain momentum and jump as high and as far as you can. Immediately after landing, jump again!

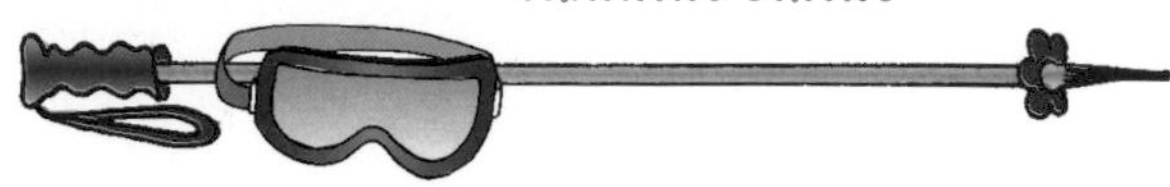

HOW FIT AM I?

Skiing is a great recreational activity. But any skier who practices a lot, prepares for competitions, races and wants to successfully participate in them knows alpine skiing is a sport! The alpine skier must be in good physical condition so he can handle the great physical strain and still have fun.

How would you rate your own physical condition? Record your evaluation on this chart and add the date. Use the second and third column to reevaluate yourself after six months and again after one year. Compare your entries to those of your training buddies.

☺ *This symbol means: Super!*

😐 *This symbol means: Mediocre!*

☹ *This symbol means: Poor!*

	Date: ________	*Date: ________*	*Date: ________*
Endurance			
Speed			
Strength			

Additional training

Make sure your training isn't one-sided but rather that it sticks to a balanced training plan. Discuss this with your trainer.

Which other sports do you do in addition to ski training? Record them on this chart. Then write down which conditional abilities they train. Mark the frequency! Surely your trainer will also give you some tips.

Sport	*Conditional abilities*	*Rarely*	*Once a week*	*Daily*

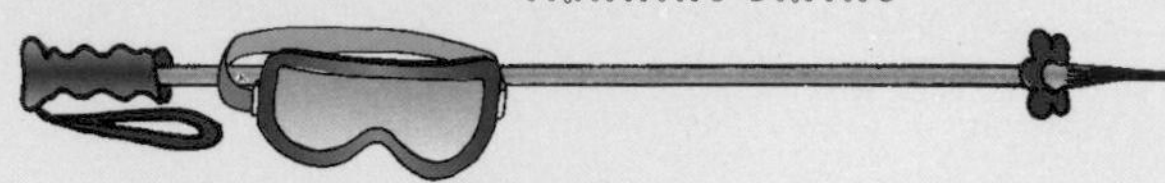

CONTROL EXERCISES

Running (endurance)

You run a predetermined distance. Choose the distance so it will take you approximately one half hour.

What is your time for that distance?

3000m Endurance run

Find a 400m track at a school or a sports arena. 3000m are equivalent to 7 1/2 laps.

What is your time for that distance?

Leg tapping (speed)

You sit on a chair with an approximately 4-inch wide mark on the floor in front of you. Now move both legs very quickly back and forth over the mark. Both feet always touch down on the floor.

How many times did you touch the floor in 20 seconds?

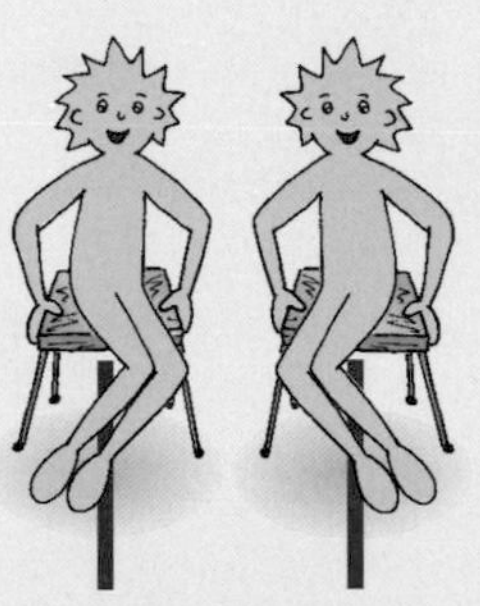

20-yard dash (speed)

This is a 20-yard sprint with a 10-yard start. Mark a distance of 30 yards. Start sprinting at the starting line, but only the last 20 yards will be timed.

How fast are you?

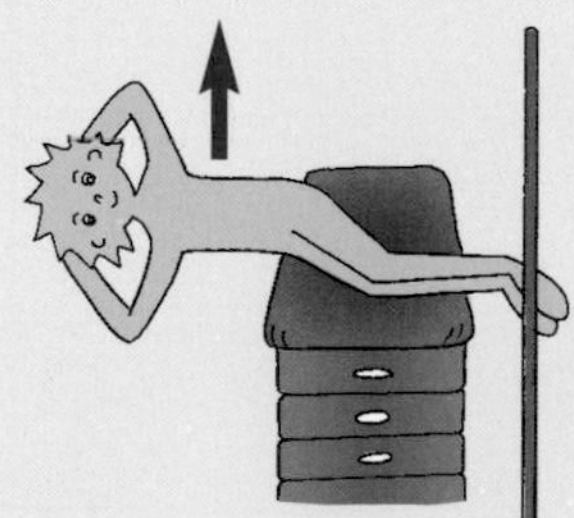

Lateral trunk raises (trunk strength)

You are lying down on your side on top of a box. Hook your feet into the wall bars. Now raise your body laterally until it is horizontal.

How long can you hold this position?

6 Sit ups (trunk strength)

Lie down on your back. Your knees are bent and your arms crossed behind your head. A hurdle approximately 4 inches above your chest marks how high you should sit up.

How many repetitions can you do?

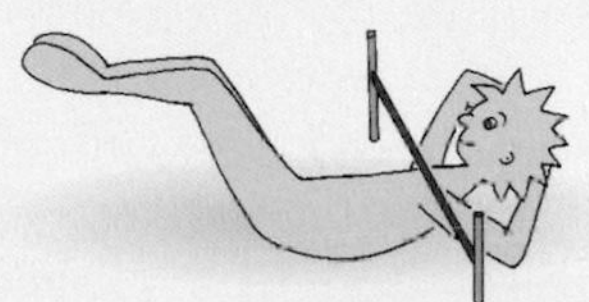

7 Lateral jumps (take-off strength)

You perform lateral jumps over a mark on a thick mat. You do this in a racing stance while holding a 2-pound weight in each hand. The mark on the side must be touched with each jump.

How many jumps can you do in 90 seconds?

8 Extended jumps (take-off strength)

You get into a starting tuck with your knees bent at a 100° angle. Now jump up and stretch really tall. Do three jumps every 30 seconds.

How long can you do it?

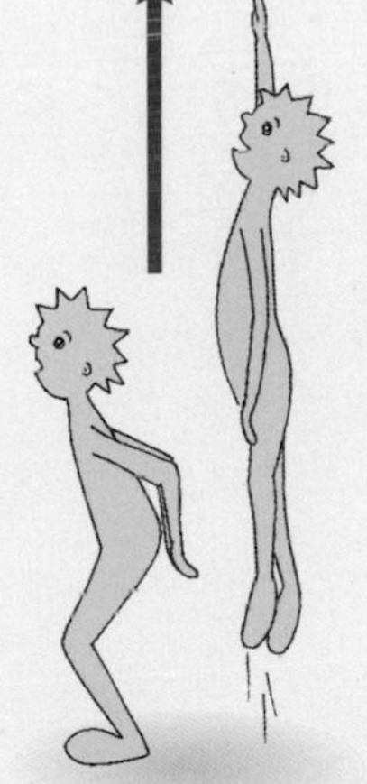

You can record your results from these and other control exercises on page 85.

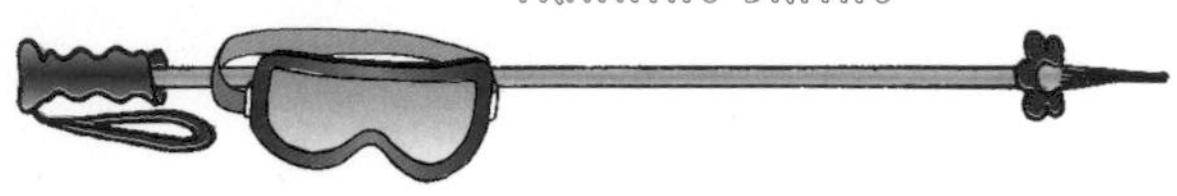

FLEXIBILITY

Flexibility is also often referred to as *agility*. Flexibility is determined by how far an athlete can flex and stretch his joints and to what degree his tendons, muscles and ligaments will tolerate a movement. Of course, this also has something to do with age and build, your strength, your coordination abilities and the elasticity of your tendons. But it is primarily a training issue.

A skier must maintain his flexibility and continue to train. It is absolutely necessary for balancing over the skis, for an ideal racing stance and an easy interplay between all of the muscles involved. You want to create a relaxed and rhythmic turn sequence, whereby your body does the necessary balancing movements.

How can you train for flexibility?

There are a number of exercises for stretching all the joints from head to toe. You will also find some of these in this book.

Don't forget to warm up before you start to demonstrate your flexibility and begin with the exercises. Cold muscles and tendons are vulnerable to injury when overstretched.

CONTROL EXERCISES

Trunk flexibility

Stand on top of a box, step, or something similar. Now bend over slowly while keeping your knees straight.

Measure how far your fingertips can reach past the edge of the box.

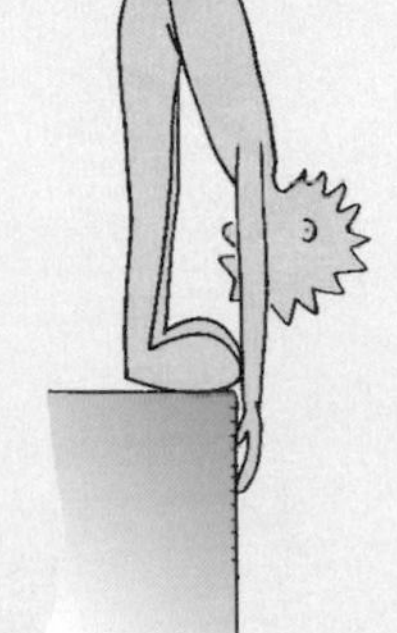

Shoulder flexibility

Lie down on your stomach. Your chin rests on the floor, your arms are extended overhead and you are holding a bar at shoulder width. Now lift the bar without bending your wrists or elbows. Your chin remains on the floor.

Measure the distance between the bar and the floor.

Splits

Do the splits and measure how far down you can touch the floor:

- *Fingertips on the floor.*
- *Palms on the floor*
- *Elbows on the floor.*
- *… keep going.*

Keep track of your performance development again with these exercises and follow our suggestions on pages 85 and 86 for recording your results.

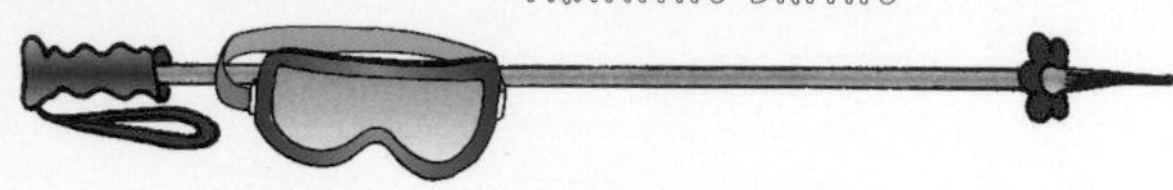

FLEXIBILITY EXERCISES

Don't forget: Don't start the exercises until you have warmed up.

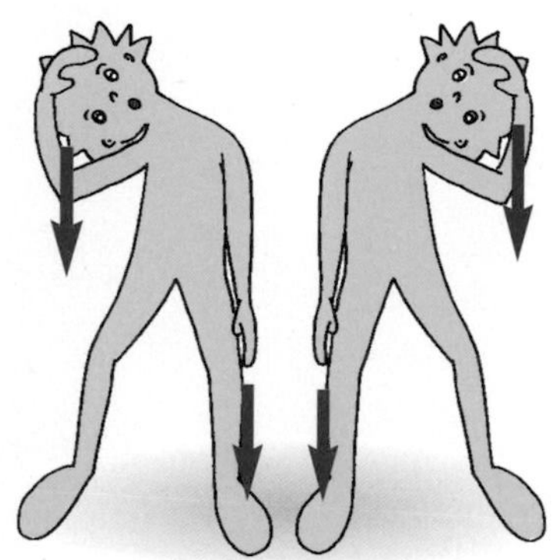

Stretching the muscles of the neck

Stand with your feet shoulder width apart and tilt your head to one side. Use one hand to gently put some pressure on the head while the other hand pulls down toward the floor. Then switch sides.

Stretching the muscles of the shoulders, back and arms

- *With the free hand reach around the opposite shoulder and push the arm back.*
- *For the second exercise, hold the arm behind the head and pull the elbow toward the floor.*

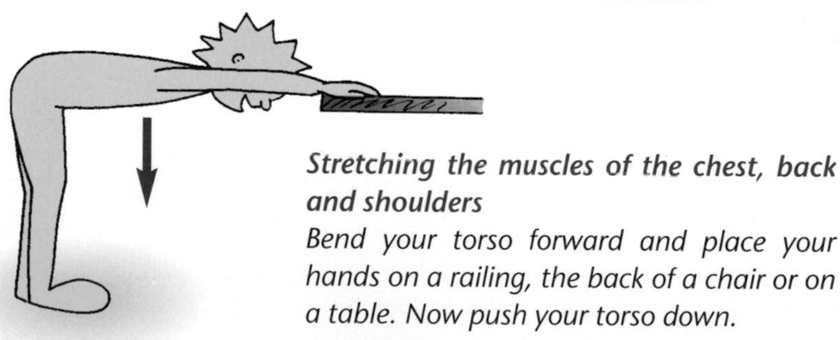

Stretching the muscles of the chest, back and shoulders

Bend your torso forward and place your hands on a railing, the back of a chair or on a table. Now push your torso down.

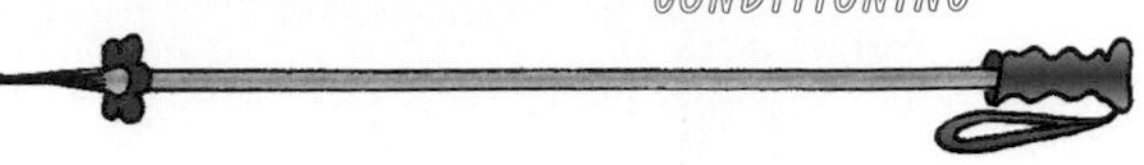

Stretching the muscles of the back

Get down on your knees and round your back like a cat.

Stretching the hamstring

Lie on your back, hold on to one leg with both hands and pull the knee toward your chest. Keep the other leg extended. Now flex both feet.

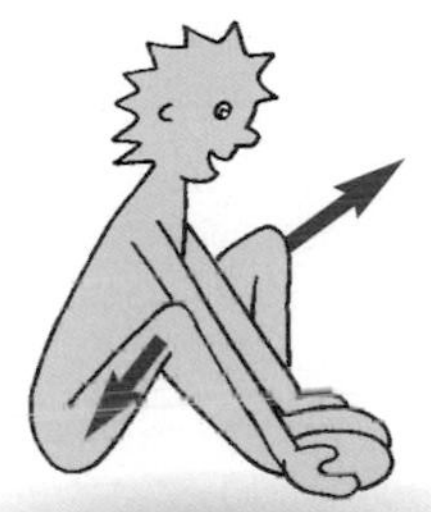

Stretching the gluteal muscles

Sit upright, place the soles of your feet together and hold them close to your body. Slowly open your knees. Now push down on the inside of your knees with your elbows, moving the knees farther apart.

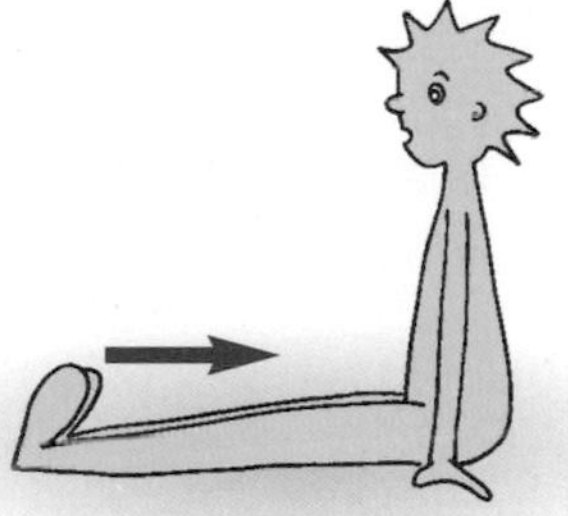

Stretching the calf muscles

Sit upright and extend your legs. Now flex your feet so your toes point toward you.

Hold each stretch for at least ten seconds. It should pull but not hurt. After training for a while, you will notice that it gets easier.

You can find many more exercises in various other books.

WARMING UP – STRETCHING – LIMBERING UP

This rule always applies, regardless of whether you are starting race training or additional fitness training, want to do exercises at home or are going to a competition! It is important that you prepare your body for the impending strain. After a day at school or a restful sleep, your muscles are relatively cold and stiff, and your breathing and pulse are still in "normal working mode." Gradually, everything is prepared for training or racing. Then, when it's time to start, your "engine" is already warmed up and you can perform your exercises with purpose and ease.

Warming up

As the word suggests, you are warming yourself up! Various exercises help to activate your muscles, increase circulation in your muscles and promote performance readiness. A sign of being warmed up is limberness, flexibility, a slight flushing of the skin and perspiration. It is a way to prevent injuries, like pulled muscles.

Any movements that get your body going are good for warming up:

Running, easy jumps, aerobics, ball games – even some slow skiing on easy runs.

All training sessions begin with the warm-up. That also goes for exercises at home, before a race or when you're late for practice. You can run a few laps or jump rope on your own.

Stretching muscles

Flexibility is improved primarily by stretching the muscles. You should never just strengthen one muscle, but always include the antagonist, the "opposing muscle."

The illustration shows a "muscle man" with a flexed arm. The muscle responsible for the flexion is the flexor, the **biceps.** That is the arm muscle you flex when you want to show someone how strong you are. The muscle responsible for the arm extension is the extensor, the **triceps**.

Feel your muscles! Try the following exercise:

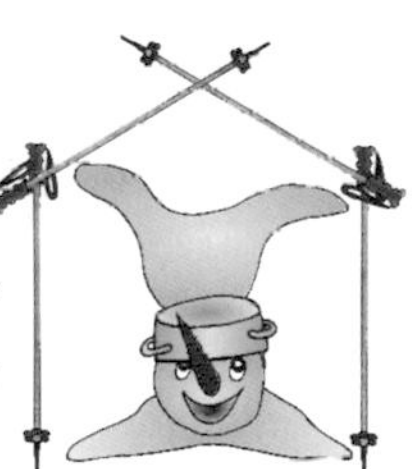

When you push down on a tabletop with your hand, your triceps is hard because it wants to extend the arm in the elbow. The biceps is soft because it is relaxed and yields. If you push against the tabletop from the bottom, your biceps is hard and your triceps is soft.

Now, try it with other "opposing muscles" on other joints like knees, hips, or on your spine with your abdominal and back muscles.

Stretching the biceps.

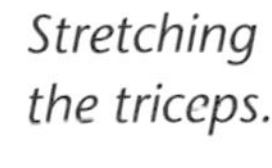

Stretching the triceps.

Here are some stretching exercises you can do after warming up. When you stretch, you elongate the muscle group you just worked. Have fun!

Stretching the front of the thigh.

Stretching the inner thigh.

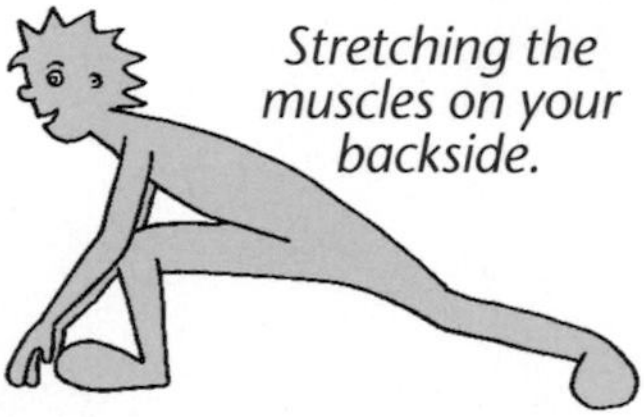

Stretching the muscles on your backside.

Stretching the back of the thigh.

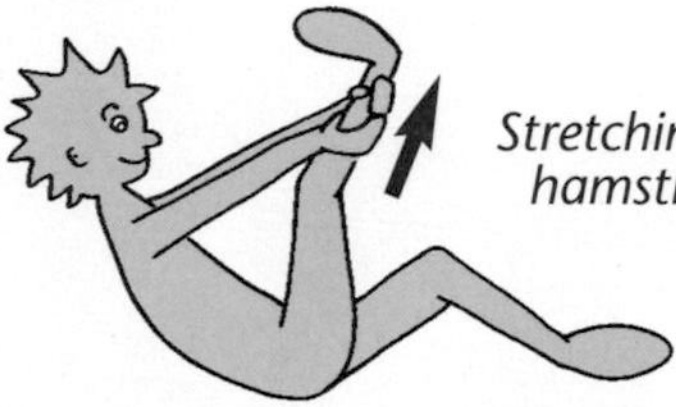

Stretching the hamstring.

Stretching the oblique trunk muscles.

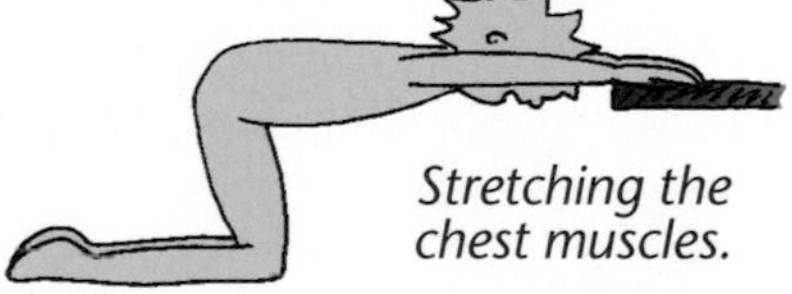

Stretching the chest muscles.

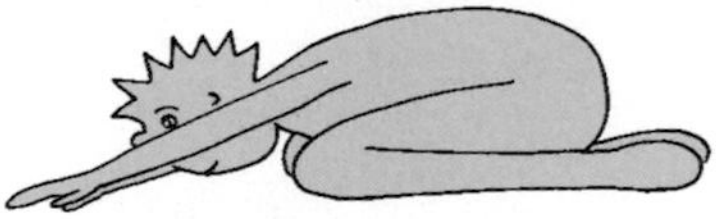

Stretching the lower back.

Count to 20 as you hold each stretch, loosen up the muscles and then repeat the stretch. Don't bounce! The exercises are intended to stretch the muscles, but they should not hurt!

Limbering up

Even though you warmed up sufficiently and stretched, your muscles are often hard and tense after a strenuous training session. Now it is necessary to limber up after you finished stretching. Most of the time, you do those exercises automatically. You shake your arms, legs and hands and gently move your joints in all directions. Some light jogging or jumping is also good for limbering up.

During this preparation phase, you did not only warm up your muscles and get your body going, but your head is also getting ready for the upcoming exertion.

In doing so, you shrug off any worries and problems, become free and ready to take on whatever is next.

TEST YOUR ABILITIES

Ski athletes who train together also compare their results. Each one wants to be the fastest and get the best time in a race. And the times quickly show how you rank.

Since an athlete's condition plays an important role, aside from good skis and perfect technique, compare each other's conditional abilities in training. Scientists and trainers have put together test exercises for alpine racing athletes. They focus on strength, endurance, speed and flexibility. With the aid of these test exercises it can be determined how well developed the physical abilities are that an alpine racing athlete needs to have. You can see how your performance evolves, how you rank in comparison with your training buddies, and which areas still show weaknesses and where you need to practice more.

On the previous pages we listed some sample exercises for the various areas. These can be done with few resources. You can do the exercises alone, with the help of a friend or with your parents. But it is more fun in a group. Surely your trainer has some ideas for additional exercises. What's important is that you repeat these control exercises in regular intervals so you can recognize the progress (hopefully not regress) in your performance.

Of course, who's the best depends on regular training. But notice that other factors also affect the result. Most often the older athlete, who has been training longer, holds an advantage over the younger one.

That is why it is of great significance to track your personal development along with your standing within the group. That's your personal way of monitoring how well you trained and whether you are improving.

PERSONAL PERFORMANCE TABLE

Number/time

Date:				
1 Endurance run				
2 3000m run				
3 Leg tapping				
4 20-yard dash				
5 Lateral trunk raises				
6 Sit-ups				
7 Lateral jumps				
8 Extended jumps				
9 Trunk flexibility				
10 Shoulder flexibility				
11 Splits				

Here you can record your results in regular intervals. Once this table is full, start a new one.

Performance graph

Exercise results, as well as all other training and competitive results, can be shown on a graph. You're probably already familiar with this type of illustration from math and science classes. If you can't get it right away, ask someone to help you. Better yet, do it together with your training group.

Get some graph paper and draw diagrams. The graduation of axis x for time can also be in weeks or months. The graduation of axis y depends on the discipline you are recording, i.e. seconds for sprinting or minutes for running, as well as the number of repetitions.

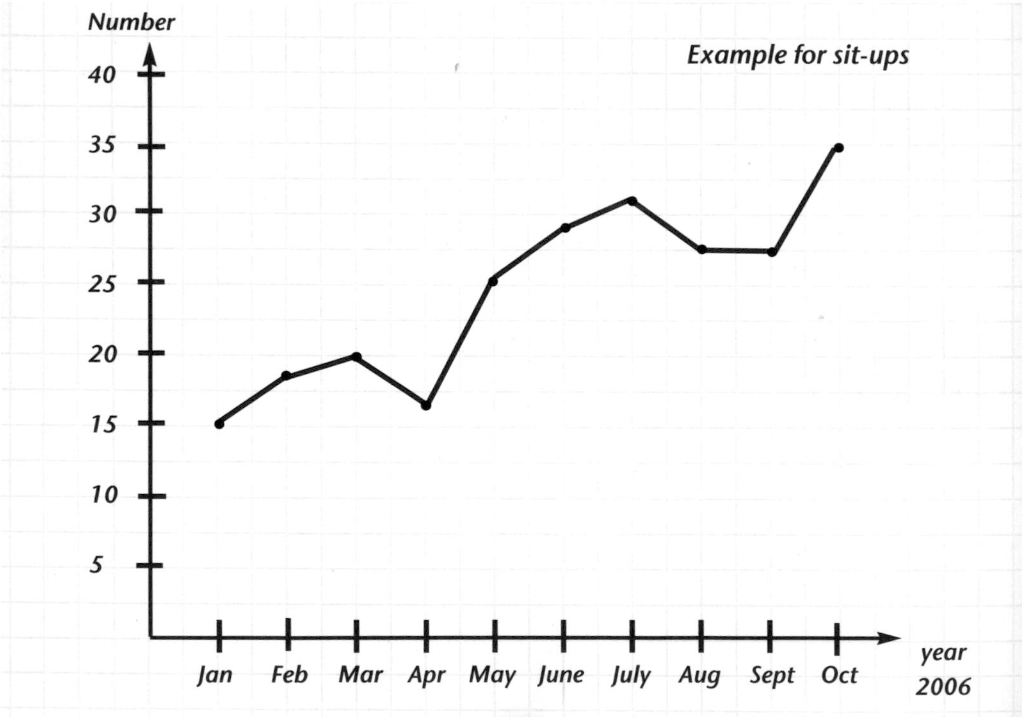

Example for sit-ups

Number

40
35
30
25
20
15
10
5

Jan Feb Mar Apr May June July Aug Sept Oct

year 2006

. . . . . 7 COORDINATION

What the snowman is showing here is just amazing. He is balancing with one hand on Skitty's head and waving with the other hand. At the same time, he is balancing a pot and pieces of coal on his feet and singing a song.

To perform such an act requires the use of many muscles and the smallest movements are coordinated with each other. He has to keep his balance and wave rhythmically, he can't lose his objects and, of course, he can't forget the words to his song. In addition, he has to keep an eye on Skitty in case he suddenly moves. And what happens if there is a sudden breeze?

The alpine ski racer moves at a high speed, making big and small turns through gates, in a tuck and sometimes with jumps.

To best perform these movements, to find the correct rhythm and stay balanced, he needs coordination.

These are specific abilities you need for skiing and, as a racer, must develop. All of the movements are subtly synchronized and adapted to the racing scenario.

In this chapter, we would like to give a more in-depth explanation of the coordination an alpine racer requires.

Sense of orientation

When the skier is on a run, a good sense of orientation is important. Your body position, the position of your skis and the surface are constantly changing. During the race, you gather a lot of information via your senses. This information is mentally processed and the racing plan is adjusted accordingly. You must learn to properly gauge speed, gradient and distances. Then you will be able to properly react in any situation.

Adaptability and adjustability

When you are skiing, the situation is constantly changing. You continuously have to adjust to varying surface conditions and adapt your mode of skiing. But sometimes unexpected situations occur: you start to slide, you touch the barrier, there is something lying on the run, you are carried out of the turn or you have a bad landing after a jump. At such a high racing speed, you don't have time to contemplate your reaction, but you must adapt to the new situation at super speed and sometimes you have to adjust your plan.

Balancing ability

It really is difficult to stand upright on a bar. By tensing your muscles and making the tiniest equalizing motions, you are able to keep your balance. The skier is always attempting to establish balance over his skis in his chosen position. Add to that the challenge that the skier is always moving, constantly changing his posture, and therefore has to continuously try to find the ideal position over the skis. In addition, there are the changeable snow conditions, varying gradient, bumps, undulations, curves, wind, etc.

How to train your balancing ability

If you train regularly, you will become increasingly more confident and will get a better feel for balancing over your skis. In doing so, you also learn to find your balance on varying surface conditions. If there is no snow, you can practice with inline skates or do special gymnastics exercises.

CONTROL EXERCISES

Lateral jumps on the balance beam (balance)

You are standing on a balance beam in a giant slalom stance. In this position, you do lateral jumps over a 4-inch wide mark, whereby you have to do one jump every two seconds. Someone else will need to dictate this rhythm (i.e., hop – hop – hop – hop – ...).

How many times can you do it without losing your rhythm or coming off the beam?

Starting tuck on the balance beam (balance)

You are standing sideways on the balance beam in a starting tuck.

How long can you hold this position?

BALANCE EXERCISES

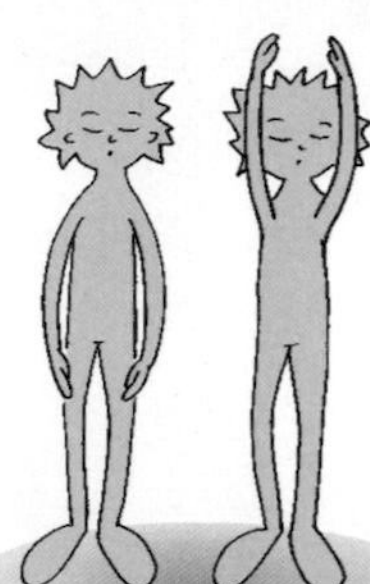

Standing up straight

Stand up straight with your legs together and your arms at your sides.

- *Close your eyes.*
- *Lift your arms to the side.*
- *Extend your arms overhead.*

Standing on one leg

- *Switch legs – first the right, then the left.*
- *Close your eyes.*
- *Lift your arms to the side and then extend them overhead.*

Standing on a shaky surface

Stand on a shaky surface and perform exercises 1 and 2.

- *Stand on a mat, a pillow or a rolled up blanket.*
- *Stand on a narrow log.*
- *Stand on a "core board" or a sports gyroscope.*

With interference

Now incorporate a few interferences into all of the exercises to make them a little more difficult.

- *Add balancing an object in your hand.*
- *Have someone toss you a ball, catch it and throw it back.*
- *Try to throw each other off balance by making each other laugh.*
- *Hold a band between you and pull. Who gets thrown off balance first?*

Other sports

Use other sports to work on your balance.

- *Riding a bicycle on uneven terrain, riding a unicycle.*
- *Inline skating/ice skating*
- *Walking on stilts/ "moon shoes"/Pedalo*

Stability ball

Sit down on a stability ball and find your balance. Of course, we will gradually increase the degree of difficulty.

- *Sit quietly, and then slowly roll to the right, to the left, backward and forward.*
- *Place a smaller ball under each foot.*
- *Bounce up and down on the ball without falling off.*
- *Create interference again by tossing a ball to a partner or pulling a band.*
- *Pull your knees up, lift your legs and lift your feet off the floor.*

Book on the head

We borrowed this exercise from ballet dancers and models. It is how they practice walking straight and elegantly. Place a book on top of your head and don't let it fall off.

- *Stand up straight, take a few steps and turn around.*
- *Walk across a soft surface and over small obstacles.*
- *Sit down on the stability ball.*

Maybe at first glance these exercises look quite easy. But try to hold each position for about one minute! You might get wobbly! Don't practice when you are exhausted but only when you are fit and alert! Maybe you can think of some more exercises.

Linking ability

As the word suggests, motions are linked together. The leg motion with canting and gliding, the body movement and the arm-pole work are synchronized.

Rhythmic ability

In alpine skiing, there are motions that always repeat themselves in the same order: canting – weighting – turning – gliding; canting – weighting – turning – gliding – ; canting – ... This is called a cycle. If this cycle is skied evenly, you can recognize the rhythm. Many recreational athletes love the feeling of skiing in a steady rhythm: swish – swish – swish – swish – ... It is hardly possible to do this when you are racing. The order of the gates, varying snow conditions, slick spots and bumps demand that you constantly change the rhythm and adapt to the conditions.

Motor reactionary ability

As any bicyclist and motorist already knows from road traffic, the higher the speed, the faster one must react to an unexpected occurrence. In alpine racing, you are usually traveling at a high speed and that is why it is important to react quickly to an unpredictable situation. If you suddenly slip on a patch of ice or there is an unexpected obstacle, you must react instantly and adjust your skiing mode accordingly, even if this deviates from your original race plan.

MUSCLE SENSE

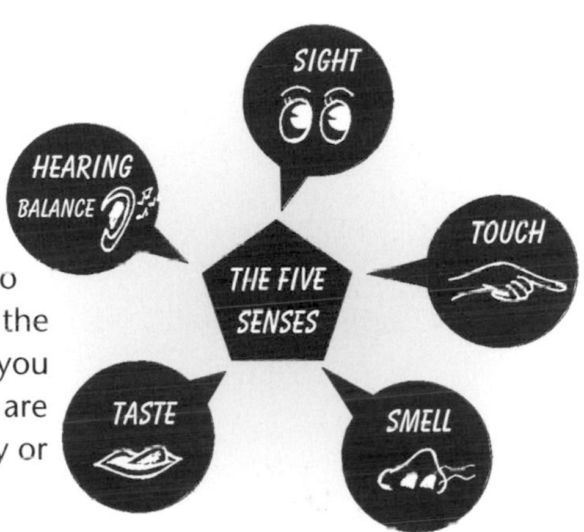

Parents and teachers often talk about the five senses you use when you are learning something new. What they are trying to tell you is to listen well, watch carefully, touch the surface, smell it and taste it. Surely you have noticed that all of the senses are not always employed simultaneously or equally.

Important senses for skiing

You definitely can't taste skiing. Smelling is more of a side effect when you have the fresh winter air in your nose or you're getting your skis waxed. We don't need to explain that you need to see to be able to ski. But you also have to be able to hear when you are racing: the rhythm of the motion, the snow and the shouts of encouragement from the spectators. Part of your ear, your hearing organ, includes your equilibrium. You need that so, in spite of the fast motions, you won't lose your balance and fall.

Some people even talk about a sixth sense. Alpine skiers really need such a sixth sense to gain a feel for muscles or motions. We just call it "muscle sense." This is very important for learning and mastering alpine ski technique. While racing, the skier watches the course, the gates and the surface conditions. He can't look to see how his joints are flexed, if he is holding the poles correctly or whether or not his skis are in the right position. You just have to have a "feel" for that. And that "feel" or that "muscle sense" is developed through diligent training.

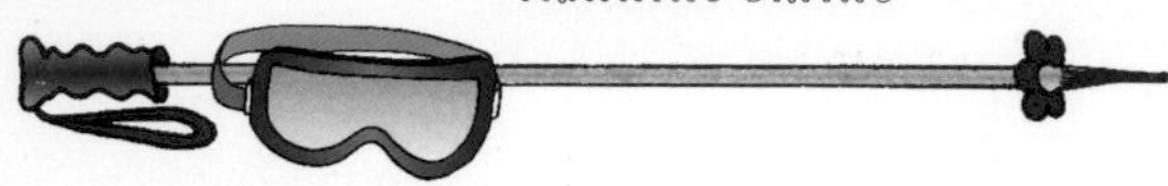

MONITORING WITH A MIRROR

You are sure that you can get into position with your eyes closed? Then use the following exercise to check!

Stand in front of a tall mirror with your ski boots on, and maybe even on skis. Close your eyes and get into a low starting tuck. Now open your eyes and check:

- *Are your joints sufficiently flexed?*
- *Are the poles close to your body and the arms at head level?*
- *Are torso, poles and floor parallel?*

Continue to use the mirror for monitoring! Your trainer and your training buddies can also serve as "mirrors."

- *Place a small object on the table in front of you. Now close your eyes and pick the object up. You have only one try!*
- *Find a large safe area. Mark a line with chalk or an object about 5 yards away and return to the starting point. Now walk with your eyes closed, then stop and open your eyes when you think you have reached the mark. Where did you end up?*
- *Take a pencil and draw a predetermined image on a piece of paper in front of you. But wait! First you must close your eyes!*

You'll have lots of fun if you do these games together with your friends.

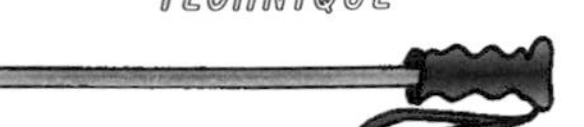

8 TECHNIQUE

Have you ever tried to juggle five apples or balls? Some acrobats use burning torches or sharp knives, which they balance while they ride a bicycle. Even the best acrobats couldn't do that when they were still in the cradle. When they first started to practice, all of the objects tumbled all over and fell down. To develop skills like these, you have to practice long and hard until you have mastered them.

A good skier must master the racing and turning techniques in the same way. Most of the time, it is the interplay between many individual small movements, that constitutes a certain technique.

You have already learned the most important techniques during your initial years as a skier, and new ones will be added throughout your continued training. Racing technique is executed so quickly, accurately and steadily, that the cycle of motions is barely perceptible and visible. Whether it was right or wrong can only be ascertained by the skier's time.

It is like our juggler. He can no longer keep track of every hand movement and every single object. The technique must be practiced until it works perfectly. If a ball or a torch falls down, it means the juggler made a mistake.

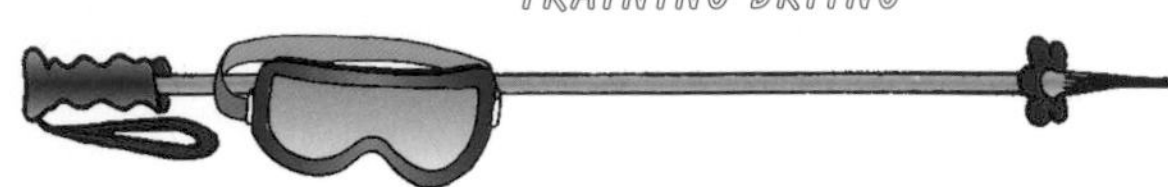

While training, you will practice the techniques and the motion sequences many times in different ways. So many times that you will no longer have to think about every single step. Imagine if you had to remember every single movement!

Like this, for example: *"glide – cant – shift weight – lean into the turn – poles back – get into a crouch!"*

You no longer have time for that while you ski. You have to focus on the course, the snow conditions and the particularities of the route.

The motions must be automatic!

TECHNIQUE TRAINING

When you are learning a new technique, it is generally introduced with an explanation and a demonstration by the trainer or ski instructor. He explains the motion sequence, tells you what to pay particular attention to and which mistakes to avoid.

As in school, there are different methods for learning. Just like people are all different, they have different ways of learning something new. The trainer will work with the different types and will use various methods to introduce new material. Often, a combination of different ways of learning is most successful.

Some of these options are:

- The trainer explains the new technique.
- The trainer or another skier demonstrates the technique.
- The new technique is shown with illustrations or progressive pictures.
- Possible mistakes are discussed with the help of images of mistakes.
- Videos are shown.
- The trainer asks the students to describe and explain the new technique.
- The students make sketches.
- The students try the new technique themselves.
- The technique is performed with monitoring and suggestions from the trainer.
- The technique is performed with monitoring and suggestions from your training buddies.
- The skiers do dry exercises without skis.

Which learning type are you? Mark those training methods that best help you learn a new technique. Try to find the best way for you!

Learning step by step

You have probably already figured out that things just don't work perfectly right away. We're not magicians! So if you want to learn something new, you have to do so step by step, from the easy to the more difficult. So at first you won't get on the steepest run, master the most complicated gate sequences and do big jumps.

Perseverance brings success

After the trainer's explanation and demonstration, it is your turn to practice the new material. Of course, it is lots of fun to learn and try out a new technique. In the beginning, the movements are rather inaccurate and you are just trying to see if your arms and legs are doing everything right. You quickly start to see progress. Your movements become more confident and faster. Your trainer will also notice. He will definitely compliment you and that will spur you on to keep practicing and continue to get better.

But gradually, all that practicing gets boring. You no longer feel any real improvements in your performance and the excitement over something new is wearing off. You think that things are going well with the new technique, so why bother practicing anymore? Now comes the point when you may not feel like training anymore. But if you quit now, you will again lose some of your skills, and all that practicing was for nothing! So remember your resolve and get past your inner temptation!

The trainer or ski instructor can't watch everyone simultaneously, so help each other! Carefully watch each other during practice runs and races. Point out mistakes and problem areas to each other and practice together.

Of course, you should and must give compliments, too!

THE ROAD TO INCREASED PERFORMANCE

After that quick progression, there will be many training days when you feel like nothing is happening. It is important to know that this phase will come. On the long road to perfect technique there are always phases of quick progression and phases of tedious drudgery. So if you think it won't get better, that you have reached your performance potential and any more practicing is useless, keep going and you will find that it will get better.

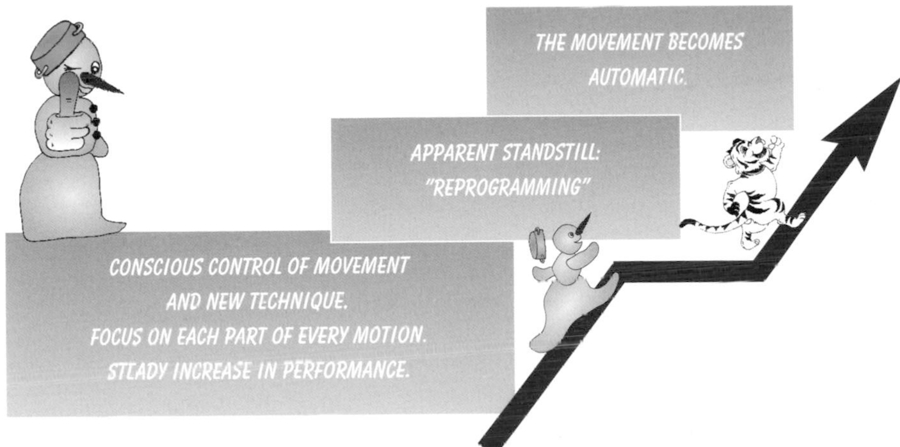

During this apparent standstill, the body prepares itself for the next step in performance development. You could say it is being reprogrammed internally for the next step. Sometimes it seems like it happens over night. So don't let an apparent standstill get you down. These are necessary transitional phases. There is only one thing to do: Hang in there! Your trainer knows this, too, and he encourage you to continue practicing diligently.

Some techniques you can learn relatively fast. For others, you may need many, many hours of training, mabe even years. You can be assured that persistent and arduous training will pay off!

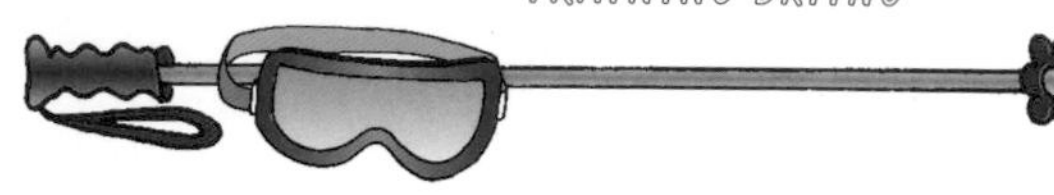

An example for learning skills:

Draw "This-is-the-house-of-Mickey-Mouse" in one stroke without lifting the pencil off the paper. The illustration on the right shows a variation on how this task can be solved. If you tried to draw it right now, you would have to really concentrate and keep referring back to the illustration. But you will notice yourself getting faster, and at some point you can even do it with our eyes closed. Now, if someone woke you up in the middle of the night you could instantly draw "the house of Mickey Mouse" without a mistake.

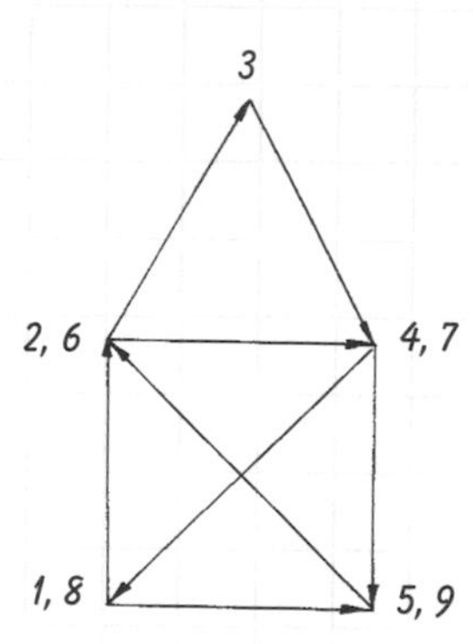

You can learn this skill relatively fast. To learn some other skills will take many, many hours of practice, and maybe even years. Just like our juggler.

Tips for technique training

Listen and watch carefully while the technique is being explained, pictures are being shown and the technique is being demonstrated!

Mentally, go over the technique again and intensely visualize the progression and movement with your eyes closed.

Practice the technique over and over while training. Check yourself after every repetition or ask others tell you what you need to work on.

Take the time to look at the pictures again and carefully go through the descriptions and compare them to your own movements. It helps if you can describe, explain or show the technique to someone else.

Monitor and help each other!

If possible, practice in varying snow and surface conditions and with different materials.

How an alpine skier must practice so a new technique works perfectly is just like learning something in school – it's different for everyone. But everyone does have to practice a lot. In the end, the technique should be executed quickly, accurately and without checking the progression, i.e. *automatically*. The many repetitions help "program" and store the progressions in your brain. Almost like loading a computer program and then retrieving it again later.

If you don't work hard in training or start skiing sloppy without concentrating, your brain will store the incorrect runs. Once something incorrect has been automated, it will take lots of effort to break that habit again later.

MONITORING – EVALUATING – IMPROVING

Don't learn and automate anything that is incorrect! That is why it is important that you monitor the progression of a new technique, recognize any mistakes and execute the movement with increasing speed and accuracy. How quickly that will happen depends on your goals and your motivation.

Julie wants to ski the new slalom course. The training group brainstormed together with the trainer about lines and technique. She paid attention and now wants to follow everything that was said. She tries really hard. The trainer watches her and then says:

"Great Julie, you are doing well!" Julie is happy and continues practicing. A few lessons later, the trainer is watching her again and says: "That doesn't look so good yet, Julie! You carry your torso too high and your skis are sliding too much!"

Now Julie is angry! She skied the course exactly the way she had a few days ago. Then, the trainer complimented her and now he's nagging!

You probably already noticed that the trainer in this story did not make a mistake. He only adapted his evaluation to the situation and the possibilities.

Julie's run in the first race was in no way perfect. But for a first time, it was quite good. Later, after many repetitions, it was reasonable to expect an improvement. The next partial goal should be reached.

On the road to fast and accurate technique, you reach many partial goals, and every little mistake is recognized and corrected. Evaluation by the trainer is best since he knows the most about skiing.

MONITORING BY THE TRAINER

On the road to fast and accurate technique, you reach many partial goals, and every little mistake is recognized and corrected. Listen carefully to what your trainer or ski instructor says and accept his advice. If ever you have a different opinion or don't understand his criticism, just ask him.

Private lessons with a ski instructor tend to get quite expensive. But in a group, the trainer can't always watch everyone all of the time. That is why you should help each other. In training, you often have to practice without monitoring. You watch yourself and decide whether it was good or bad. A skier must be able to do that! Remember your trainer's suggestions from recent practice sessions.

During the explanations, Tom was doing something else and now he has to stay after training and practice an additional 10 minutes with the trainer. Is that a fair punishment?

HAVE YOU HAD A LAUGH TODAY?

"What's going on with you, Paul?
You always seem so sleepy during training!"
"Not to worry, Trainer!
That's just the great talent resting deep inside me."

Everyone is going off the little jump, except for Tina.
The others yell: "Are you chicken?"
"No way! But sometimes you have to be able to control yourself!"

Two skiers collide on a run and get tangled up. One yells,
"Help, help, I can't feel my leg!"
Answers the other one: "Of course not if you keep pinching my leg!"

Sometimes it's good to "kid around" a little!

. . . . 9 GLIDING, CANTING, TURNING

The skier must continuously adapt to new situations while he races downhill, does the Super-G, the giant slalom and the slalom. He skis on flat and steep terrain; sometimes he makes short and narrow or big wide turns, and he constantly has to deal with varying snow conditions.

That is why, over the years, and with the experience of the best ski athletes, an ideal technique has been developed and was proven to be the best. Every young skier should learn it and then adapt it to his own abilities. Based on this ideal technique, every top athlete tries to find the best technique to meet specific demands. These differ in ski position, body position, canting, pole use, etc. But there are no set rules. As a skier you learn to continuously adapt to any given situation and to adjust your technique accordingly.

Ski instructors, trainers and scientists continue to think about which racing technique might be the best and therefore the fastest. That's why there are always innovations and changes in execution. We have illustrated and described the current prevailing forms. But what matters for you is always what your trainer or ski instructor says. If sometimes you don't understand his opinion or his way of doing things, just ask him about it. He will give good reasons for his opinion. If you like, you can also make notes or draw sketches at the respective place in this book.

BODY POSITION

Many joints are responsible for keeping the body securely positioned over the skis. You can see them in this drawing. When you are racing, you don't remain in a rigid position like the skier in the drawing. You continuously change your position – sometimes more, sometimes less. The responsible joints balance every change in body position, thus always reestablishing a balanced position.

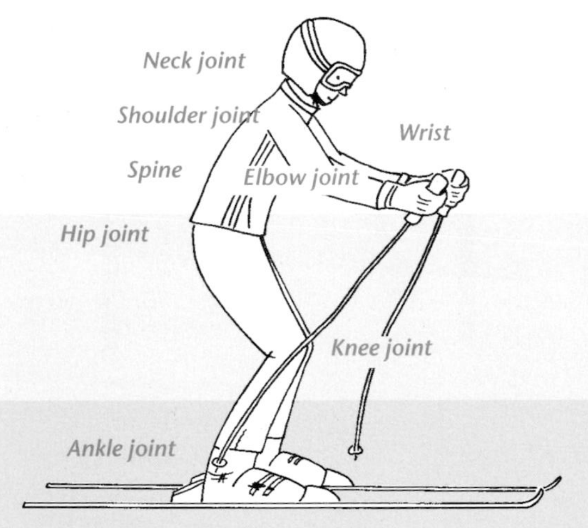

You use these joints to make the fine adjustments to stay balanced over the skis.

You use these joints to make the larger adjustments to stay balanced over the skis.

To adjust the body's position over the skis, the ankle joint is the most important.

Observe yourself! Assume the starting position. Now bend your hips more. You can see that in order to keep yourself from losing your balance, you automatically flex your knees and ankles more. If you bend your hips less and stand more upright, then ...

....

....

Basic position

This position is the starting position for all other techniques in downhill, slalom or giant slalom.

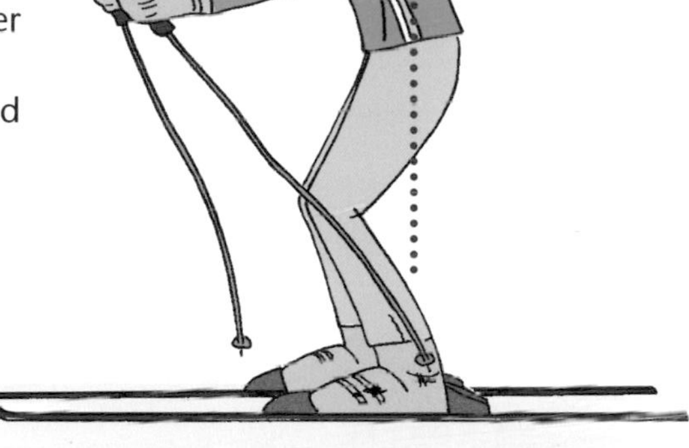

This is how it's done:

- All joints are flexed or slightly flexed.
- The center of gravity is over the middle of the foot.
- The arms are held forward and to the side.
- All the muscles are tensed.

Low position

This position is the basic position for skiing fast in flat terrain, for Super-G and downhill. The low body position makes it easier to keep you balance. But a lower position also requires more strength than a higher one.

This is how it's done:

- All joints are flexed.
- The arms are held out front.
- Body tension is high
- The ski stance is wider.

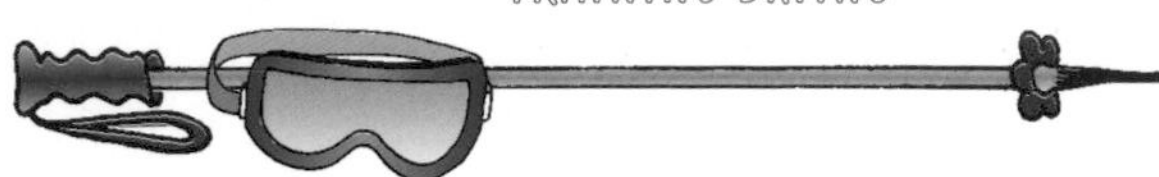

Gliding

The highest speeds are achieved while gliding in a racing tuck. You quickly assume this position whenever the course arrangement permits. That's the case during downhill and between longer turns.

When you glide in a racing tuck your body position is very low, so your body is more aerodynamic.

This is how it's done:

- The back is slightly curved.
- The joints are heavily flexed.

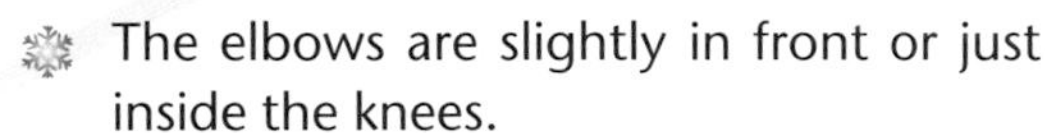

- The elbows are slightly in front or just inside the knees.
- The arms are held in front of the head.
- The poles are tucked under the arms.

- ***Weight is distributed equally between skis.***
- ***The center of gravity always lies over the center of the foot.***

- The lower legs are parallel.
- The skis lie flat (no edging).

- The torso, the poles and the skis are parallel.
- Upper and lower legs are approximately at a right angle to each other.
- Lower legs and skis are approximately at an acute angle to ach other.

- *If the run has a lot of undulations, don't flex your upper body as much so the legs have room to balance the movements.*
- *When approaching an undulation, lean forward some to straighten your legs a little to avoid lifting off.*
- *Move your upper body back a little when you come out of an undulation so your body doesn't get so compressed. The legs absorb the pressure.*

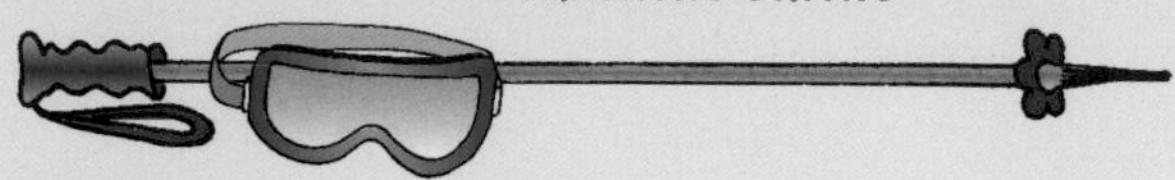

The skiers in these drawings are skiing downhill in a tuck. What mistakes are they making?

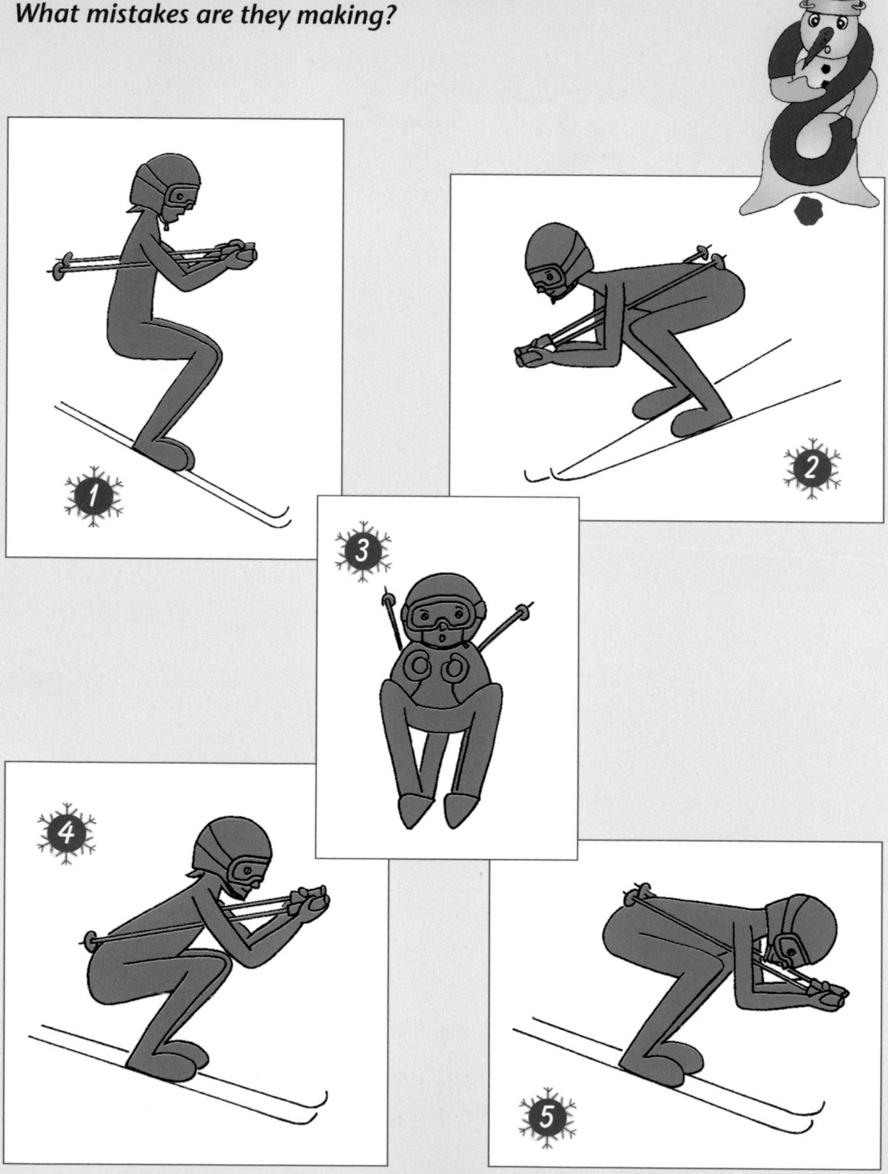

1

2

3

4

5

BASIC RACING TECHNIQUE

The slicing turn, which is made possible by the particular shaping of the carving skis, is the basic turn for all racing disciplines. Once you have mastered the basic technique, you can adapt it to the various racing situations and disciplines and adjust it accordingly.

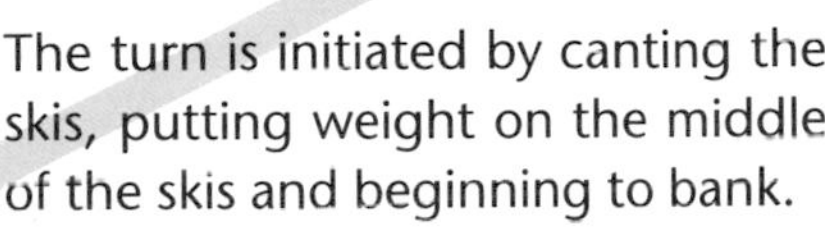

The turn is initiated by canting the skis, putting weight on the middle of the skis and beginning to bank.

The speed increases between turns. The skies lie flat and glide. The body is in the advantageous crouch position.

In the next turn, the skis are again set on edge and flexed.

This is what you have to pay attention to:

Body position:

- *Medium to low crouch position.*
- *Keep your balance by moving the torso forward – back, high – low and sideways.*

Arm-pole action:

- *Arms and poles are held laterally in front of the body.*
- *Arms and poles keep the balance and maintain the rhythm.*

Steering:

- *If possible, turn on the waist of the skis.*
- *Legs determine the setting of ski edges.*
- *The torso controls banking.*
- *More weight on the outside ski.*
- *Hips remain neutral.*

Ski position:

- *Skis are parallel and open.*
- *Ski edges are set evenly.*
- *Skis are level.*

Joining turns:

- *Turning rhythm remains steady.*
- *Joining of turns is fluid.*

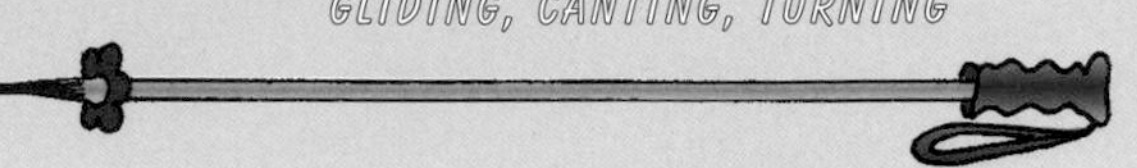

Do you recognize the mistakes the skiers in these drawings are making?

These mistakes can also occur in the basic racing technique:

- Skis slip.
- No rhythm.

Are you familiar with these mistakes? Do they sometimes happen to you? Mark the ones you still have to pay attention to. (Use a pencil so you can soon erase your check marks!)

Slicing turns – downhill and Super G

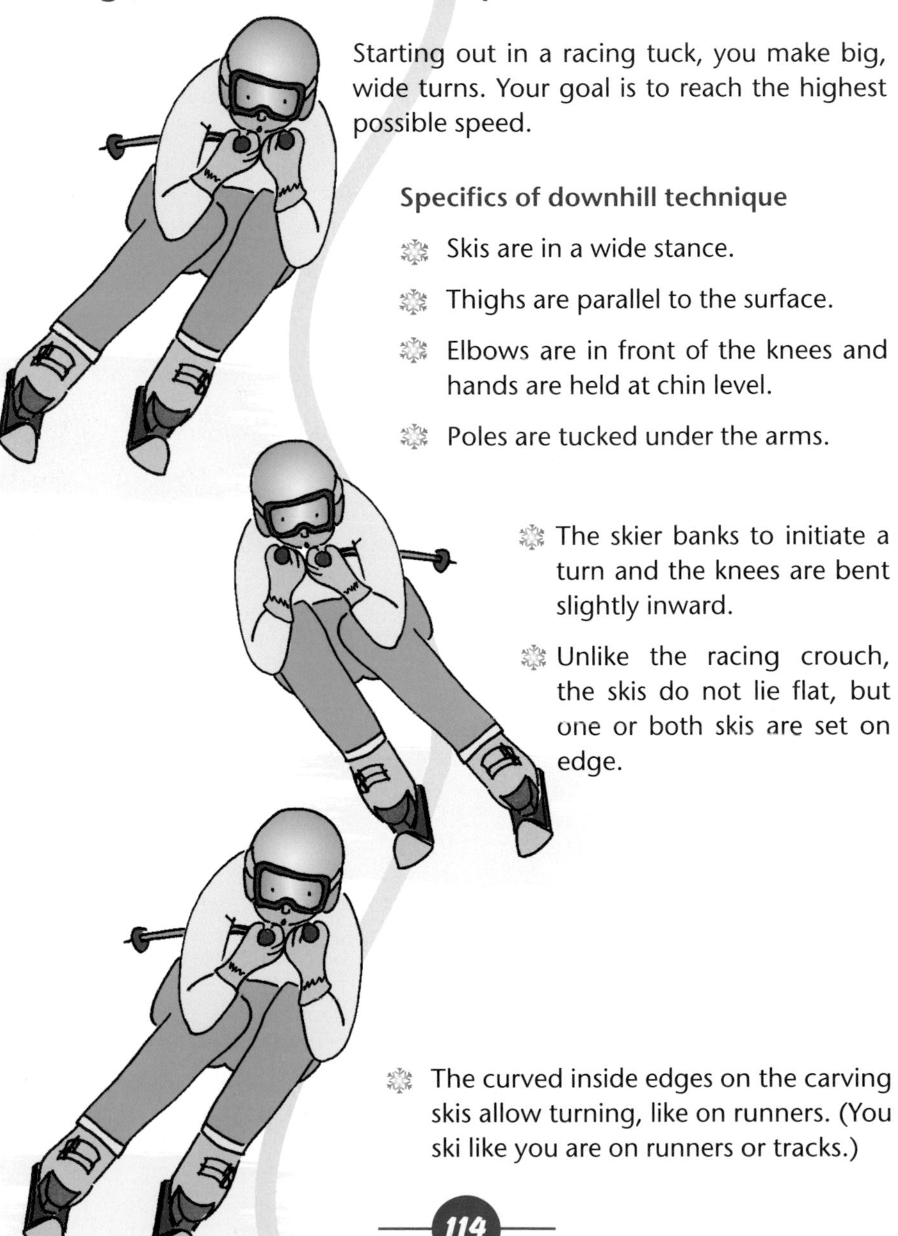

Starting out in a racing tuck, you make big, wide turns. Your goal is to reach the highest possible speed.

Specifics of downhill technique

- Skis are in a wide stance.
- Thighs are parallel to the surface.
- Elbows are in front of the knees and hands are held at chin level.
- Poles are tucked under the arms.

- The skier banks to initiate a turn and the knees are bent slightly inward.
- Unlike the racing crouch, the skis do not lie flat, but one or both skis are set on edge.

- The curved inside edges on the carving skis allow turning, like on runners. (You ski like you are on runners or tracks.)

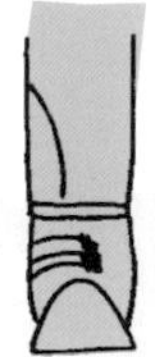

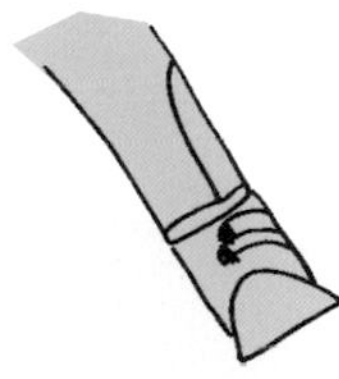

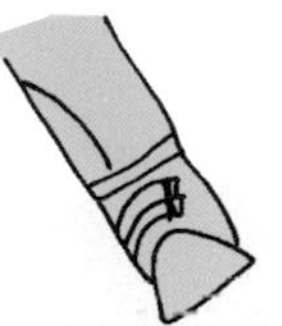

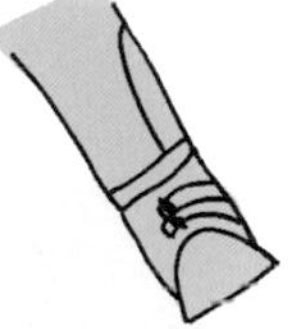

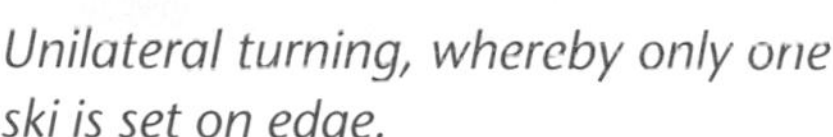

Unilateral turning, whereby only one ski is set on edge.

Bilateral turning, whereby both skis are set on edge.

Do you recognize the mistakes the skiers in these drawings are making?

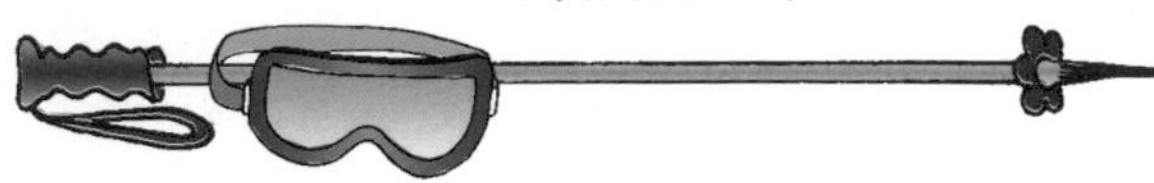

Slicing turns – giant slalom

The turns are no longer as long and often it isn't enough to rely strictly on the track type carving.

Specifics of giant slalom technique

- The body stays in a low position. The muscles are tensed.
- The skis are parallel. Open, wide ski stance.
- Arms are laterally in front of the body and go along into the turn.

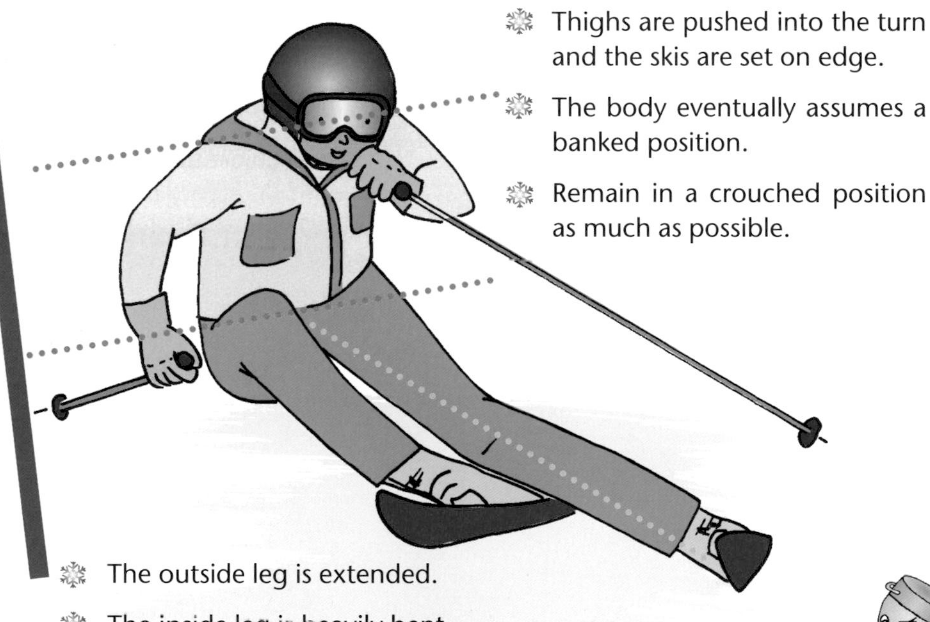

- Thighs are pushed into the turn and the skis are set on edge.
- The body eventually assumes a banked position.
- Remain in a crouched position as much as possible.

- The outside leg is extended.
- The inside leg is heavily bent.
- At the pole, arms are held together.

Due to the higher centrifugal forces, additional balancing motions with the torso are necessary.

WHAT HAPPENS IF ...?

There are some typical mistakes that skiers practicing giant slalom technique frequently make. We have listed some of these here. Write down the effects these mistakes can have on the progression of a race.

What happens if the ski stance is too narrow?

____

____

What happens if the torso is carried too high?

____

____

What happens if the skis slip?

____

____

What happens if the arms hang down?

____

____

What happens if the torso initiates the turn?

____

____

Slicing turns – slalom

The fastest movements are executed during the slalom. The turns and directional changes occur in quick succession.

Specifics of slalom technique

- The body is carried in a medium to higher position.
- The ski stance is parallel, open, but somewhat narrower.
- Heavy arm pole action. The gate poles are tilted with the ski poles.

- Aggressive turning from outside ski to outside ski.
- Movement is initiated with the legs. The torso stays motionless.

WHAT HAPPENS IF ...?

There are also some typical mistakes that skiers practicing the slalom technique frequently make. Write down again how these mistakes can affect the progression of a race.

1 *What happens if* the ski stance is too wide?

2 *What happens if* the torso is bent back too far?

3 *What happens if* you put weight on the inside ski while turning?

4 *What happens if* the outside arm is extended too far forward?

5 *What happens if* the gate pole is not tilted with the arm?

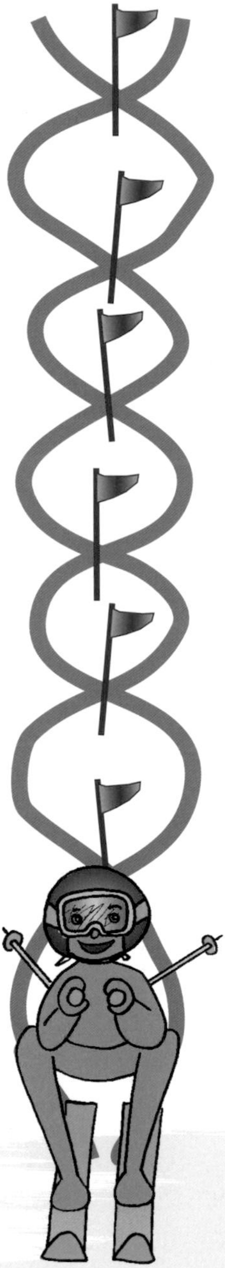

Oh, gosh! Always so much excitement before a race! What's the fastest way to the restroom?

LEARNING FROM MISTAKES

Aside from the technical descriptions, we have also highlighted a number of possibilities for mistakes in this chapter. Images and descriptions of mistakes are important learning tools for training and practicing. It is also important that, as friends and training buddies, you observe each other and call attention to each other's technical mistakes.

There are many places in this chapter with images or descriptions of mistakes. Mark your own "problem situations." Use a pencil so you can soon erase your marks.

What does your trainer or ski instructor bring to your attention?

....

....

Sometimes it can be good to deliberately make mistakes. It's the best way to feel the difference between a flawed and a perfect skiing technique.

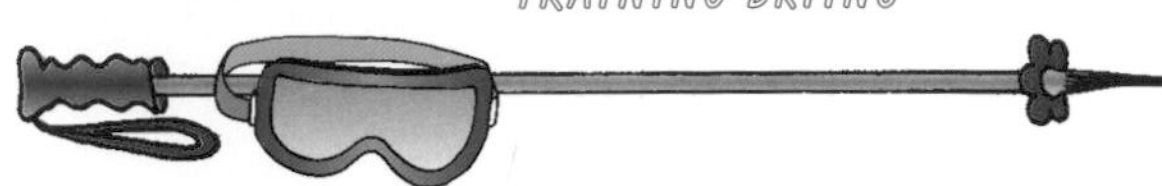

Good training buddies train together and have lots of fun together, too.

You think you are doing everything right and you are still being criticized? Do the others "have blinders on?" Or do you maybe see yourself incorrectly, i.e., have a false image of yourself?

How about a video recording? You can leisurely watch your run and identify good technique and problem areas.

What matters is that you don't see the basic racing technique as a rigid stance. It is the basic form that you adapt according to the course and the conditions. Here are a few suggestions for practicing that adaption.

THIS IS HOW YOU CAN PRACTICE:

Turning with varying ski positions
Sideways

- *Wide, narrow or closed ski position.*
- *Stem position or scissor position.*

Lengthwise

- *Stride position.*
- *Telemark position.*
- *Level skis.*

Skiing over undulations or bumps

- *Wide stance.*
- *Narrow stance.*
- *Closed stance.*
- *Stem position.*
- *Scissor position.*

Skiing with varying materials

- *Turning with "Big Foot."*
- *Turning with unbuckled ski boots.*
- *Turning with cross-country skis.*
- *Summer training with inline skates.*

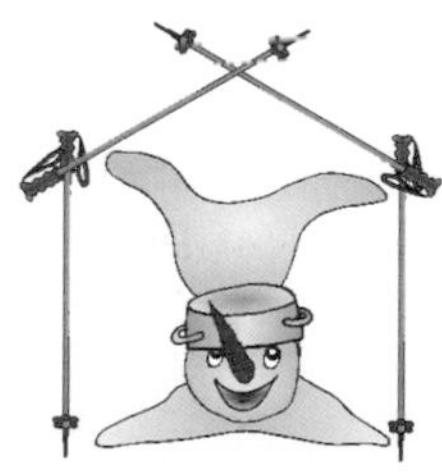

Try yourself out! Deliberately depart from the norm and observe yourself. How does your body position change? How well is the ski moving? How good is your balance?

THE START

You feel in top shape, have prepared well for the race, and of course you are extremely tense. Now comes the start and your run begins. That should be like an explosion. The start has to give you the right momentum for the race and shave off important seconds.

A super start gives you self-confidence for your race, whereas a "goofed up" start can quickly take away any hope of winning. Therefore, don't forget to regularly practice your starts.

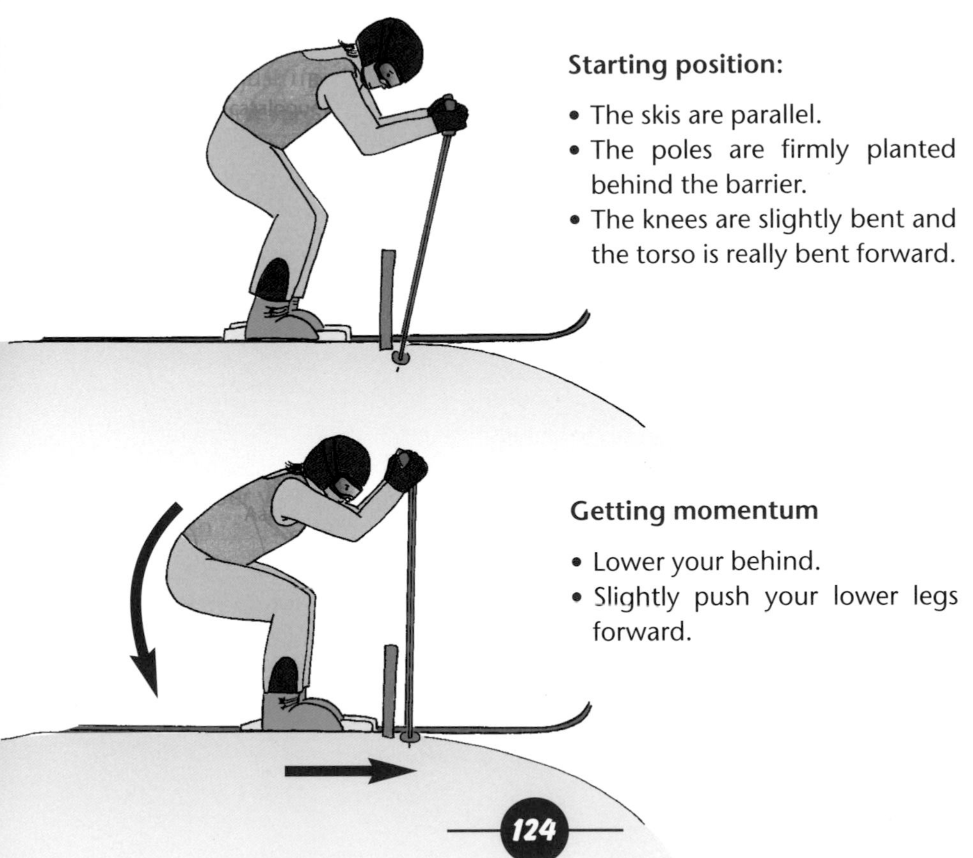

Starting position:

- The skis are parallel.
- The poles are firmly planted behind the barrier.
- The knees are slightly bent and the torso is really bent forward.

Getting momentum

- Lower your behind.
- Slightly push your lower legs forward.

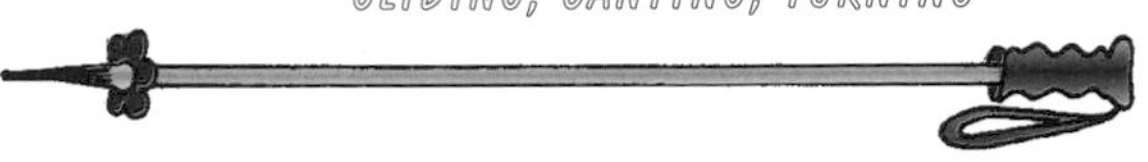

Pull start

- The trunk and arm muscles are very tense.
- The body is pulled with its entire weight over the poles and pulled forward with the arms.
- As soon as the skis pass the poles, the arms are extended forward.
- Now you begin to skate while pushing off with both poles.

Catapult take-off

- The body quickly becomes very erect.

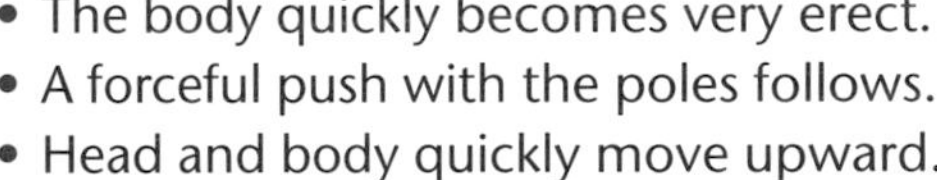

- A forceful push with the poles follows.
- Head and body quickly move upward.
- The legs kick back and up.
- The body leans extremely far forward.
- Now the legs swing catapult-like through the barrier.
- Begin skating.

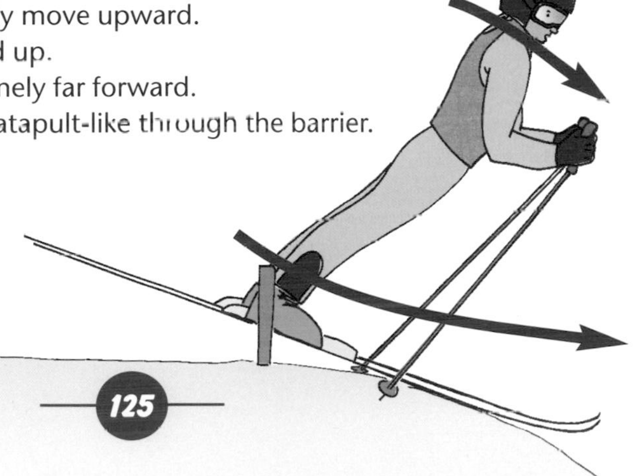

... JUST A FEW TIPS

As the name suggests, the track a sliced turn makes should be a crisp line. Look at your track. Can you see a clear impression from the ski edge or do you see evidence of sliding?

Did you know...

... that experiments with narrower waist skis were already being done in the 1970s?

... that during the 1980s giant slalom skis with a narrower waist were being built for the world class skiers?

... that carving skis did not become hugely popular until the 1990s?

Have you ever thought about how carving skis work? What effect does the waist have? Why does the ski make a curved line when it is set on edge? Try a little experiment.

Cut the shape of a carving ski out of stiff paper. Lay a piece of thin paper over our drawing and trace the outline. On a piece of construction paper trace around this stencil and cut the carving ski out.

Set your paper ski on its edge and bend it so the entire edge is touching down. Now ski on that edge. It works best on carpeting.

........10 KEEPING THINGS STRAIGHT

Almost all things in people's lives are regulated. What chaos would there be if everyone everywhere could do whatever he or she wanted, whenever they wanted? Certain rules apply when living together as a family or learning in school. Traffic laws regulate road traffic and every game has rules.

Skiing is done in a special environment that must be protected and taken care of. In addition, ski racing is a very fast sport and therefore poses a particular danger. There are important regulations every skier should know and obey so everyone will have fun, no one gets hurt and the environment is protected, too.

Find out about rules on the slopes and in lift areas. People who love nature also work for its conservation!

THE FIS RULES OF CONDUCT FOR SKIERS AND SNOWBOARDERS

Consideration for other skiers and snowboarders

Every skier and snowboarder must conduct himself or herself in a manner that does not endanger or cause damage to others.

Controlling speed and manner of skiing/ snowboarding

Every skier and snowboarder must ski/board at sight. He must adapt his speed and manner of skiing/boarding to his abilities, the terrain, and the snow and weather conditions.

Choosing a track

The skier/snowboarder coming from behind must choose his track so he won't endanger a skier or snowboarder in front of him.

Passing

Passing is allowed from the top or the bottom, from the left or the right, but only at a distance that leaves the skier or snowboarder being passed plenty of room for movement.

Merging, starting and going uphill

Any skier or snowboarder who wants to merge onto another run, restart after stopping, or move uphill must always look uphill and downhill to make sure that his action will not endanger others.

Stopping

All skiers and snowboarders must avoid making non-emergency stops at tight or blind spots on a run. Skiers or snowboarders who have fallen down must vacate that spot as quickly as possible.

Climbing up or down

Skiers or snowboarders who want to climb up or walk down a run must do so along the edge of the run.

Observing signs

All skiers and snowboarders must observe the markers and signals.

First aid

In case of an accident, all skiers and snowboarders are obligated to assist.

Obligation to carry identification

In case of an accident, every skier and snowboarder is obligated to identify himself, regardless of whether he is involved or a witness.

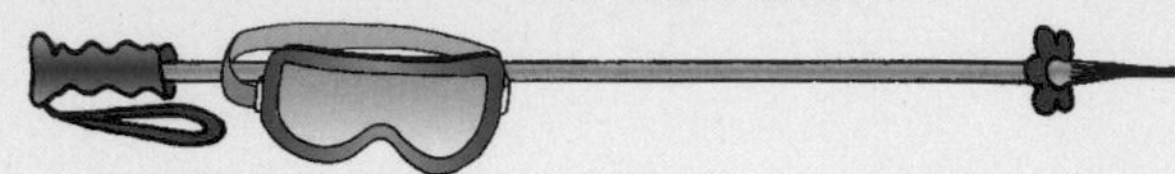

Just like in road traffic, there are hazard and prohibition signs posted on the runs and lift poles. The symbol easily clarifies the statement.

Write down the meaning of these two signs.

Find out about other signs that make you aware of dangers and noteworthy situations!

What do you think about the snowman's attitude?

HEY, YOU CAN'T JUST THROW THAT SODA CAN IN THE SNOW! PUT IT IN THE WASTE CAN OR TAKE IT HOME!

IT'S NOT A PROBLEM! SOON IT WILL SNOW AGAIN AND YOU WON'T BE ABLE TO SEE IT ANYMORE!

SKIERS ARE NATURE LOVERS

Not many athletes are lucky enough to be so close to nature. As a skier, you experience the beauty of the mountains, the snow and the healthy crisp winter air.

But there are many nature lovers who perceive the increasingly popular sport of skiing as a threat. They believe that young plants are destroyed by skiers coming down the slopes, that the animals are disturbed by all the activity and that the ski tourists leave lots of trash behind. But that's not necessary. If every skier and snowboarder is considerate and respectful, loves nature and cares about its preservation, there can be a happy coexistence.

The FIS environmental regulations

The FIS has established environmental regulations for winter sport athletes. Derived from those, we have listed the most important ones here:

- Get information about your ski area.
- Support the resorts in their care for the environment.
- Choose environmentally friendly modes of transportation, such as bus or train, to get to the ski area.
- If traveling by car is necessary, form car pools.
- Only ski or snowboard if there is a good snow cover.
- Stay on the marked runs.
- Observe markers and stay off closed runs.
- Abstain from skiing/snowboarding off the runs, particularly in wooded areas.
- Don't ski/snowboard in protected areas.
- Be careful of animals and plants.
- Don't litter!

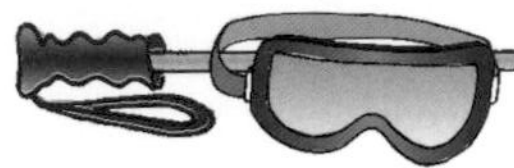

Food pyramid

Cakes, pastries, filled chocolates, chocolate, candy

Milk, cheese, yogurt, sausage, meat, eggs, beans, peas, nuts

Bananas, apples, oranges, kiwi, carrots, tomatoes, lettuce, broccoli, cucumber, peppers

Bread, potatoes, rice, pasta, granola, cereal

Water, juice and water mix, tea

Here you can see which foods you should consume in large quantities (bottom) and which ones you should rarely eat (top).

There are examples listed from each food group.

Find 15 fruits and vegetables – horizontal, vertical or diagonally, forward and backward!

O	P	R	M	P	O	T	A	T	O	E	S	E	B
Z	U	C	C	H	I	N	I	W	L	T	M	R	I
S	V	N	M	Y	L	M	S	C	I	W	O	T	X
Q	D	M	G	Y	R	O	C	I	H	C	W	F	Z
U	M	R	E	B	M	U	C	U	C	Y	U	O	I
A	N	A	P	R	T	Y	M	O	W	O	K	T	H
S	X	N	W	S	G	V	L	R	N	M	P	A	C
H	I	A	V	K	G	I	Y	U	C	X	W	F	A
X	Z	N	A	P	P	L	E	M	S	E	Z	M	N
S	N	A	R	W	H	L	E	T	T	U	C	E	I
K	Z	B	P	E	P	P	E	R	S	K	T	W	P
P	E	A	R	W	C	A	R	R	O	T	L	S	S
G	R	A	P	E	S	W	F	L	E	M	O	N	I
K	I	W	I	Y	R	R	E	B	W	A	R	T	S

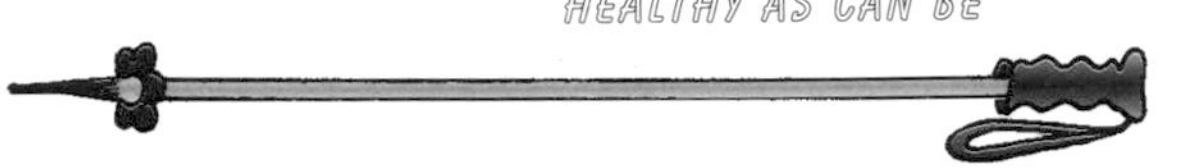

. . . . . . 11 HEALTHY AS CAN BE

Anyone who thinks that hard, sweaty training several times a week is enough for athletic success will soon learn that that's not the case. Aside from the demanding training, recovery phases are very important, as well as plenty of sleep, healthy nutrition, good hygiene, organization and much more.

You should be familiar with your internal clock and learn to pay attention to it. It will tell you when your body is particularly efficient and when you urgently need rest and should relax. A good skier can also tell when he needs high-energy nutrition to stay efficient and focused.

In this chapter, we have compiled some interesting information on that topic. Use this as an incentive to familiarize yourself with your internal clock and healthy nutrition.

Have fun!

Late morning

Afternoon

Midday

Morning

Night

OUR ACHIEVEMENT POTENTIAL

As you can see on the above curve, our achievement potential experiences highs and lows in the course of the day. It is similar for most people, and we have adjusted our lives accordingly. Most school instruction is done in the morning, then some people even take a nap at lunchtime. In the afternoon, we accelerate again, and at night, our bodies gets its well-deserved sleep. Anyone who follows this rhythm lives a healthy and productive life. You can feel it if you don't get enough rest and sufficient sleep, and it would be a shame not to use those "highs."

Eat and drink yourself fit!

Athletes who eat or drink too much, or the wrong thing, before training or a race are not efficient. They feel stuffed and appear tired and listless. Many bodily functions slow down because the stomach is working overtime. But we must eat and especially drink to replenish the body's used-up energy and to balance the loss of fluid caused by sweating. It is also necessary to do so periodically during long training sessions and competitions.

Take from this overview what is most suitable for your main meals, snacks, and the in-between energy boost, and what isn't. Choose your foods and drinks, as well as the time of consumption, so you are sufficiently satiated during training or at a competition, but are not still digesting.

How long foods stay in the stomach until they are digested:

Approx. one hour:	*Water, tea, broth.*
Approx. 2 - 3 hours:	*Cocoa, banana, apple, roll, rice, cooked fish, soft-boiled egg, whole grain bread, cake, bread and butter, granola, vegetables.*
Approx. 4 - 5 hours:	*Sausage, meat, fried potatoes, French fries, beans or peas.*
Approx. 6 - 7 hours:	*Layer-cake, mushrooms, fish in oil, fatty roast.*

If you sweat, you have to drink a lot

To balance the loss of fluid from sweating, you have to drink enough fluid during training and at a competition. Otherwise, your efficiency level will drop, the blood thickens and absorbs less oxygen, and that leads to muscle cramps.

- **Suitable beverages before and after exertion**
  Water, juice and water mix in proportions of 1:3, lightly sweetened beverages.

- **Suitable beverages after exertion**
  Water and juice mix with a higher proportion of juice, milk smoothies, beverages with higher sugar content.

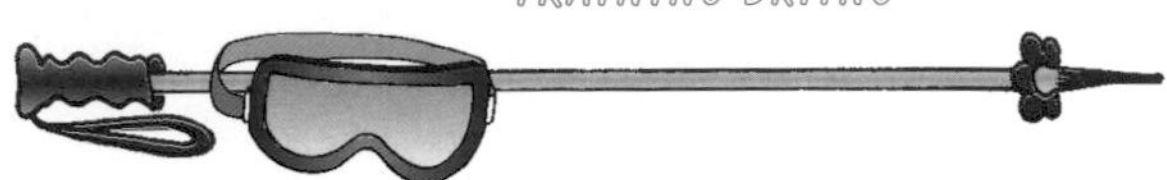

Energy sources

You are only capable of extreme physical exertion if you intake sufficient energy (sugar/starch) in the form of nourishment. If you have absorbed a sufficient amount, you achieve optimal efficiency. Not enough causes a drop in efficiency, lack of concentration and fatigue. But with too much energy absorption, there is a danger of extreme nervousness and quick exhaustion.

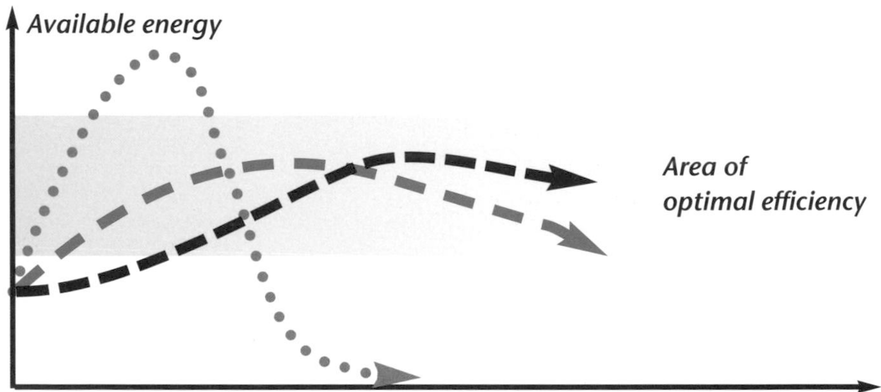

• • • • • • • *Sweets, honey, grape sugar and sweetened beverages give you a quick burst of energy and thereby a fast performance boost. But it doesn't last long.*

— — — *Milk smoothies or apples give you quick energy that is also available over a longer period of time.*

— — — *Granola, whole-wheat products and bananas don't give you an immediate energy boost, but that energy is available over a long period of time.*

ABOUT MUSCLE SORENESS

Are you familiar with this? You get out of bed the day after training and everything hurts? Every step is painful, and no one can touch your upper arm or your thigh? Ouch! You can't sit down either. When you tell your trainer about this he'll say, ***"You have muscle soreness!"***

When does muscle soreness occur?

Whenever you work your muscles particularly hard or in an unfamiliar way, you can get muscle soreness. The muscle just hasn't gotten used to the new strain. Whenever you do unfamiliar exercises, go back to training after an extended break, or train especially hard, the chances for getting muscle soreness are pretty high. Muscle soreness is not a beginner's affliction, but can occasionally hit the performance athlete, too.

What exactly is muscle soreness?

When an exercise is new to your muscle or you have been kind of lazy, then the muscle doesn't remember exactly how the exercise is done. It is called "experiencing a loss of muscular coordination." These unfamiliar muscle movements cause tiny injuries to the muscle. The emergence of pain-causing substances leads to the painful tightening of the muscle. The cause is tiny tears in the muscle fiber.

Why does muscle soreness begin the following day?

It isn't the unfamiliar strain that causes muscle soreness, but rather the emergence of fluid in the muscle caused by the mini-injury. That doesn't happen immediately, so you only feel the pain on the following day. Unfortunately, it usually lasts a few days.

What do you do when you have muscle soreness?

Muscle soreness appears quickly and disappears slowly! It takes time for the muscle to repair itself. A sore muscle needs rest and protection, so the tiny injuries to the muscle fibers can heal. Sit in a sauna or take a bath,

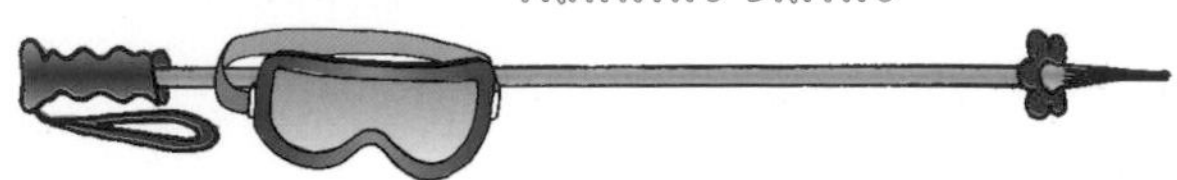

because heat helps soothe sore muscles. Massages or exposure to infrared light also work. Besides that, you can actively do something for your painful muscles. Do some easy limbering exercises or stretches like the ones we described. But the exercises shouldn't hurt.

Should I train with sore muscles?

You can continue to train in spite of muscle soreness. Go easy on the affected muscles and focus instead on other areas. For example, if you have sore leg muscles, you can do primarily arm exercises in fitness training or focus on theoretical instruction.

How can you avoid muscle soreness?

Muscle soreness can occur particularly easily when cold muscles are strained. So don't forget to warm up and stretch! In addition, every exertion should begin gradually and then be increased. If you have not been able to train for an extended period of time, start to train slowly and don't overdo it. However, your best protection is to avoid long breaks between training sessions!

Muscle soreness is not an illness!

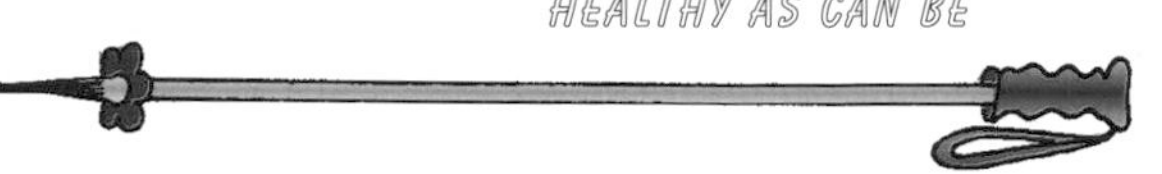

ACCIDENT PREVENTION AND FIRST AID

There are many things you can do to enjoy your favorite sport without getting injured. We have pointed this out repeatedly in the book. It includes:

Equipment
Skis, ski boots and bindings must be in good condition and coordinated. You can probably do the basic maintenance yourself, but every so often you should consult a professional. He can give you various protective wear: helmet, goggles, hand protection, and knee protection.

Physical condition
There is a reason why we devoted an entire chapter to conditioning. Skiing safely requires an all-around well-trained body. That includes honing all conditional abilities, like endurance, strength, and flexibility. Having command of the technique and good coordination and balance are important. Pay attention to your body's signals and warm up before training and racing.

Knowing the rules of conduct
People who don't observe the resort regulations have no business being there! Alpine skiing is a fast sport and not without danger for the athletes. Obeying the rules, being cautious and considerate is important (see pages 128-129).

Seeing clearly

If you wear glasses, it is important to have that vision aid on the slopes. Many accidents happen because the athletes can't see clearly. They cannot make out distances, obstacles and peculiarities of the slopes or have difficulty doing so until it is too late, and they are not able to react quickly enough. Also, protect your eyes from the sun, wind and snow.

In case of ailments

You enjoy skiing, you want to win races and be a winner. Therefore you train regularly and with determination. But nevertheless, the body sometimes doesn't cooperate. If you are in pain or have other physical problems, visit a specialist and get a real diagnosis. A thorough examination will determine what the problem is and you will get tips for special training.

Most of the time, an injury does not mean total rest from training. There are various strength exercises you can do while still resting the affected body part. Discuss it with your physician and the trainer.

If something does happen

Every skier is obligated to give assistance to an accident victim. That includes:

... securing the site of the accident

Make people aware of the accident site by posting a skier or a pair of crossed skis 10 to 20 yards uphill from the accident site. This will give timely warning to subsequent skiers and keep them from skiing into the accident site.

... giving first aid to the accident victim

Take off the victim's skis and make him as comfortable as possible. You can learn the first steps for CPR and first aid for accident victims in a first aid class. Make sure the victim does not get too cold lying in the snow.

... getting help

As quickly as possible call the trainer, the ski patrol, or emergency medical assistance. As the first person on the scene, your intervention is very important, but then a professional must quickly make the correct diagnosis and give treatment.

Every athlete should regularly take a first aid class. Maybe you can discuss this in your training group and practice first aid procedures.

By the way, knowing about first aid isn't just important in skiing, but also in a family, in traffic, on vacation and in many other areas.

I took my last first aid class on: ....

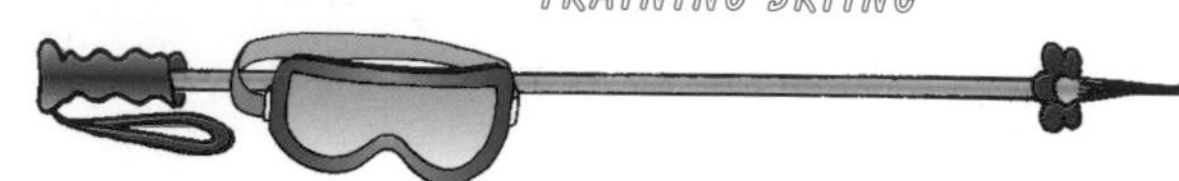

"Is the weather report reliable?"
"Sure, but the date isn't always correct!"

The teacher explains:
"Frostbitten body parts are
rubbed down with snow!"
Asks Tony: "And in the summer?"

. . . . 12 SOLUTIONS

P. 31 **1.** Tell your trainer that you are still unsure and afraid. Surely he will start you off with some easier tasks.

2. Tell him that you are already quite good at that and would like to practice something more difficult.

P. 46 **1.**

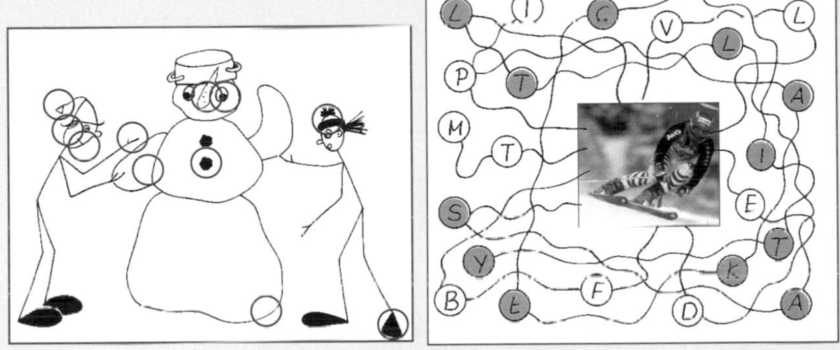

2. The American host city for the Olympics was Salt Lake City, Utah.

P. 56 **1.** The little hat-bug unfortunately does not reach his sweetheart.
2. 1 – four skiers, 2 – one skier, 3 – no, 4 – blue, 5 – red and white barricade

P. 57 **Our opinion:**
Self-confidence – enjoys skiing – ~~self-doubt~~ – ~~blind anger~~ – risk taker – ~~impatience~~ – laid back – ~~fear of making mistakes~~ – ambition – competitiveness – confidence in one's ability – ~~pessimism~~ – ~~bad mood~~ – feeling in good form – alertness – concentration.

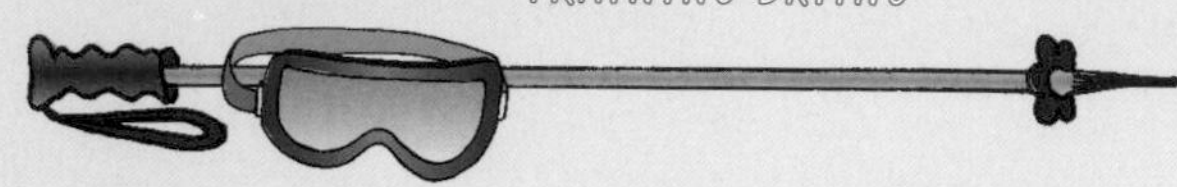

P. 62-63

15 – 18 points

With your attitude about sports, you can really go far. You enjoy competition, are fair and have willpower. Keep it up!

10 – 14 points

You have a pretty good attitude about sports, but sometimes you are stuck in first gear. With more fun and competitiveness, you could be more successful.

6 – 9 points

You mostly think about yourself! You need to work on your attitude about fairness and comradeship. Take training and racing seriously, be fair to other athletes and have more fun with skiing.

P. 66

S	W	I	M	M	I	N	G	T	M	O	P	L	X	H
H	F	C	R	O	S	S	C	O	U	N	T	R	Y	G
I	G	E	L	R	U	I	M	W	S	I	N	N	E	T
K	N	S	F	E	S	N	O	T	N	I	M	D	A	B
I	I	K	F	P	T	G	N	I	L	C	Y	C	I	B
N	E	A	X	E	R	E	C	C	O	S	Z	W	B	U
G	O	T	V	L	X	S	N	I	U	K	P	U	T	E
X	N	I	H	L	Z	R	Y	R	T	N	C	P	M	W
J	A	N	R	I	G	K	F	M	I	W	Z	Q	N	X
H	C	G	M	N	W	I	L	L	A	B	D	N	A	H
J	U	D	O	G	N	J	O	G	G	I	N	G	B	X
N	V	S	O	G	Y	M	N	A	S	T	I	C	S	L
T	Y	B	Y	W	L	L	A	B	Y	E	L	L	O	V
B	I	G	N	I	T	A	K	S	E	N	I	L	N	I

P. 103 Additional training is not a punishment but rather a reward. Because if you can do additional training, you get more help to improve your performance.

P. 106 … you also decrease flexion in the other joints.

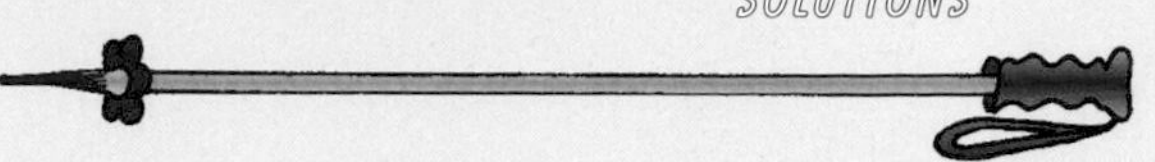

P. 110 Mistakes in racing tuck

1 The body is too erect.
2 The skis are not parallel.
3 The skis are not gliding smoothly but are on edge.
4 The center of gravity is too far back.
5 the skier is not looking ahead.

P. 113 Mistakes in basic racing technique

1 the body position is too erect.
2 The angles of legs and hips are so awkward that the torso is bent too far forward.
3 The poles are "hanging".
4 The ski edges are not set consistently, so the legs form an x.

P. 115 Mistakes in downhill

1 The skis are not on edge.
2 The poles hang down.
3 The torso is too erect and not parallel to the skis.

P. 117 What happens if ...? Mistakes in giant slalom

1 It becomes difficult to set an edge and it's hard to balance.
2 Incorrect banking makes the turn initiation more difficult and edge pressure is too weak.
3 The turning rhythm is lost and the ideal line abandoned.
4 The turn is initiated too late.
5 The turn is over-rotated.

P. 119 What happens if ...? Mistakes in slalom

1 The legs have to work too hard and the turns are not rhythmic.
2 An incorrect base position leads to incorrect turn execution.
3 Too much sliding occurs, leading to a loss in height and speed.
4 It causes rotation and the turn becomes over-rotated.
5 It causes threading, the possibility of falling and disrupts the rhythm.

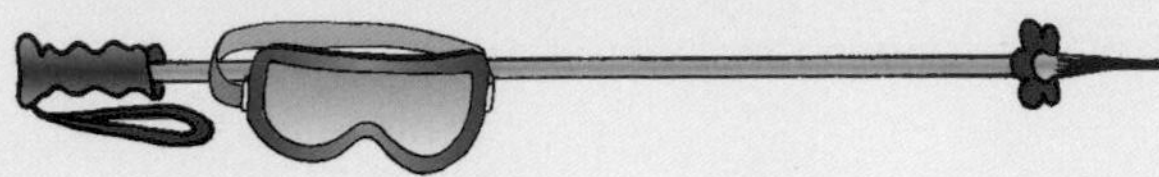

S. 120

P. 130 **1 Caution, intersection!**

This means that another run, a lift or a road intersect a run. Sometimes the sign is accompanied by a symbol or an explanation.

2 Caution, danger!

Here you have to be particularly alert!

P. 130 Anything you bring to the slopes you can also take home with you, or at least to the next trash can! The snowman is apparently not thinking about what the slopes will look like next summer, without the snow!

S. 132

O	P	R	M	P	O	T	A	T	O	E	S	E	B
Z	U	C	C	H	I	N	I	W	L	T	M	R	I
S	V	N	M	Y	L	M	S	C	I	W	O	T	X
Q	D	M	G	Y	R	O	C	I	H	C	W	F	Z
U	M	R	E	B	M	U	C	U	C	Y	U	O	I
A	N	A	P	R	T	Y	M	O	W	O	K	T	H
S	X	N	W	S	G	V	L	R	N	M	P	A	C
H	I	A	V	K	G	I	Y	U	C	X	W	F	A
X	Z	N	A	P	P	L	E	M	S	E	Z	M	N
S	N	A	R	W	H	L	E	T	T	U	C	E	I
K	Z	B	P	E	P	P	E	R	S	K	T	W	P
P	E	A	R	W	C	A	R	R	O	T	L	S	S
G	R	A	P	E	S	W	F	L	E	M	O	N	I
K	I	W	I	Y	R	R	E	B	W	A	R	T	S

. . . . 13 LET'S TALK

DEAR SKI PARENTS!

It is easy to become enamored with skiing. It is simply a wonderful winter sport and for many people, it is the best recreational activity in the snow. Nature and speed are fascinating, and together with friends it's twice as much fun.

Your child has also learned to ski and is having fun. But now he is no longer satisfied with the basics and pure recreational enjoyment, but wants to practice skiing as a real sport. He wants to train seriously in a club and maybe even be part of a good team. Do you know why? Ask your child or have him show you the page in the book that lists the motives. But you can assume one thing: Anyone who trains in skiing wants to be successful, wants to start in races and win.

This book on training is for young skiers in their first years of training. It offers them lots of information about the sport, about conditioning and fitness training, about technique, coordination, and how to train correctly. These young people will learn to better realize their own potential and to use their bodies more consciously. This does not only promote more effective training, but also prevents possible over or under training.

The basic and intermediate training are the same for all young skiers, regardless of whether they later continue to ski recreationally or aim to ski among the world's best. The book provides good orientation and support for successful training to all.

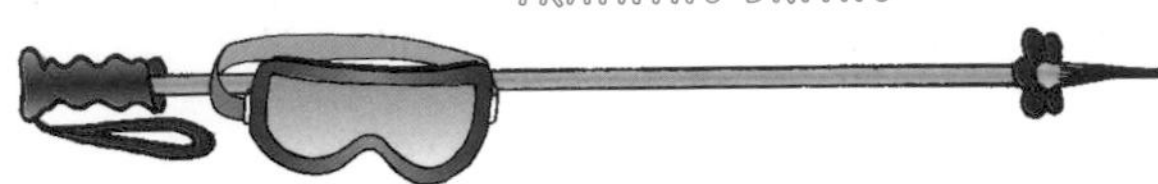

All parents, siblings, grandparents and friends receive important information. In today's world of television, computers and other modern media, many of our children and adolescents don't have enough exposure to books, particularly specialized books. So don't expect that your young skier will be able to immediately understand the contents on his own. Use this book together with your children as a training companion, workbook and reference book.

You might occasionally be asked to help with designing performance charts, too. Enjoy the young skiers' progress and racing successes along with them. The children need our approval, praise and recognition. Be sympathetic on those occasions when things aren't going well. Not everyone has what it takes to be a world-class competitor.

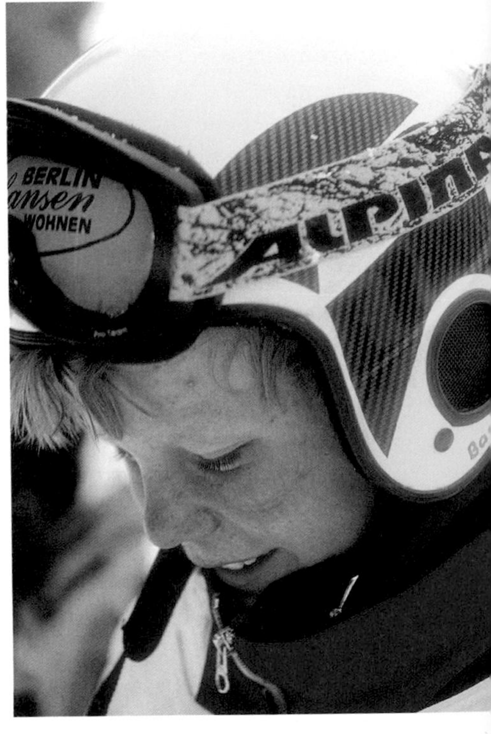

More than anything, competitive sports are fun, promote social interaction, develop ambition and perseverance. As they train together, children and adolescents learn to overcome their inner weakness and learn how to deal with success and failure.

Character traits, such as fairness, dependability, punctuality, organization, perseverance, the willingness to take risks, courage and team spirit, are cultivated and will also be useful in all other areas of life.

DEAR TRAINER!

Good youth training focuses on the entire personal development of children and adolescents. It is considered a learning activity because it promotes control and automatic control processes. It has a socializing effect because group training in particular practices social norms, rules and behavior patterns. Training for children and adolescents is stimulating and takes moods, perceptions and feelings into account.

It ensures positive experiences, allows for needs and wishes, is conducted in a warm, loving and open-minded atmosphere. The young skiers are your partners in this – providing they are actively involved in the training process and have enough freedom to act. Therefore, don't view the young athletes as recipients of your orders, but as partners in the mutual training process. Tell them why, when and which exercise is necessary for them to do, and which training load is particularly appropriate for which areas of training.

We would like to hereby hand the children a workbook that is a training companion. They can review things they have learned, as well as record goals they have set, motives and their personal performance development. Seize the opportunity to read certain chapters together, assign small tasks to be completed at home, fill out charts and compare the results. Performance diagrams are a good way to document and follow training achievements.

Of course, no book is a substitute for the years of experience a trainer has. Also, sometimes the opinions of trainers, sports scientists and book writers can differ. View this training book as a training supplement and as an aid in the involvement with the sport beyond the mutual training.

A good youth trainer always thinks about how he cannot only use ski training to teach about the fall line and technique, or develop conditioning, but how he can actively involve children and adolescents in

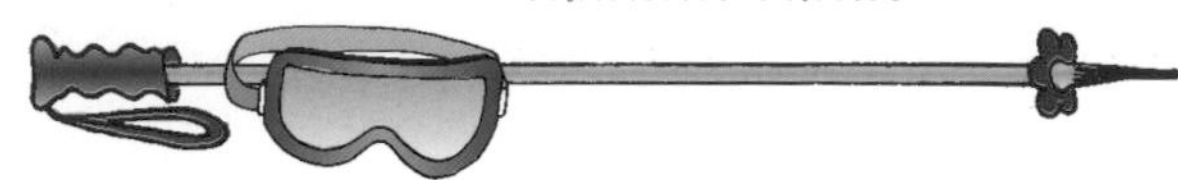

the practice- and training process to be able to, aside from improving the quality of practice sessions, consciously foster the personal development of his athletes.

We always welcome tips and suggestions.

We wish you and your protégées continued fun and success.